Cybercrime does not discriminate. Be warned that anyone, anytime, and anywhere is fair game.

# SOCIAL ENGINEERING AND DIGITAL DEFENSE SURVIVAL GUIDE

# GUIDE FOR THE EVERYDAY PERSON



**Disclaimer:**

This book was written with the intent of helping readers better understand some of the tactics and strategies social engineers use to access information for nefarious purposes and is for educational purposes only. The techniques discussed in this book are based on the authors' experience as well as research during the time this book was published. All of the websites depicted in this book are from public and private domains and are available to anyone with access to the Internet. The authors and publisher specifically disclaim any liability, loss or risk, personal or otherwise, that is incurred as a consequence, directly or indirectly, of the use and application of any of the contents of this book. We will not be liable for others' actions directly or indirectly; do not attempt any of these social engineering examples in the book.

# Table of Contents

# A Word From
# HENRY AND JIMMY

**hy We Wrote This Book . . .**
Many years ago, we were attending a DEFCON, an internationally respected information security conference, where we were advised to turn our phones off and not bring credit cards to this hacker conference.

Now for people in marketing (like Jimmy), the phone is critical to our way of life. For marketing people, conferences are for gathering information, building relationships, and growing your network. There was no way a marketing person could attend a conference and not use their phone.

On the drive to the DEFCON conference, we started talking about ways to lock down phones, digital privacy, and how to protect yourself from unwanted visitors. A few weeks later, we got together at our favorite coffee hangout and started talking about the conference and all the fun we had. We thought, why don't regular people know about all this? At that moment, we decided we wanted to create a book for the regular person, from students in school to senior citizens and everybody in between. This book was created out of our sincere desire to simply help people.

America is always socially under attack. During this time, our nation has watched a president go through impeachment trials, civil unrest, and the impact of COVID-19 on our daily lives. From celebrities to ex-presidents, hacks are happening everywhere. Even social media giants like Twitter have been compromised. In 2020 one of the biggest social media attacks of all time hit Twitter. Now more than ever, it is important for one to be aware of the realities of social engineering and how to defend yourself digitally.

The United States Federal Bureau of Investigation (FBI) Internet Crime Complaint Center (IC3) recently issued its 2021 Annual Report. We encourage you to read this report for yourself at www.ic3.gov. In 2021, the IC3 reported 2,300 complaints daily, with financial losses exceeding $6.9 billion. This represents a 93% increase in total complaints from 2020. Later in the book, we will share more insights from this report. The bottom line, this report demonstrates that many people in America are victims of cyber-related crimes.

It is truly no longer a question of "IF" a cybercrime will happen to you, but "WHEN." People are using a variety of scams through the devices we use every day. Each day we read various threat intelligence reports that share with us one breach after the other, from school systems to government offices to hospitals to your family. If you don't believe us, go visit www.informationisbeautiful.net and search for "World's Biggest Data Breaches & Hacks. You will see some familiar organizations.

As we have seen countless times in the movies, most hackers hide in the shadows and can do really bad things to an organization or person by hacking their technology. There is another kind of hacker we want to introduce you to in this book. This hacker accesses what they want by simply talking and manipulating people directly or maybe through a message on a social platform. The term in the technology community is a social engineer. The social engineer is a part hacker and part con artist. There are three kinds of hackers, so you are tracking: White Hat, Grey Hat, and Black Hat. White hats are the proverbial "good guys," and black hats are the bad guys. Grey hats are a mix between white hats and black hats.  A moral compass is critical in this field of work.

For many of us, our parents shared with us from an early age things to do to keep us safe in our world. We remember our parents teaching us not to take candy from strangers or get in a van or car with unknown people. Even if they promised to take me somewhere, like an arcade or the movies, we don't ever go. We realized that some people reading this book may not know about arcades. In a time long before the Internet, iPods, Xbox, Switch, and Playstation, people would go to an arcade and play video games. For some of us, it was hanging out at the Putt-Putt Arcade, which also had a putt-putt golf course.

The world has changed a great deal since our childhood in the 80s. Today's parents need to warn their kids to be aware of online predators, cyber criminals, and social engineering attacks. There are many kinds of cons criminals will try. It is important for you, your family, your business, and your community to understand how to keep safe in our current technological world, where we are constantly interconnected and susceptible to many "cyber-strangers."

For many of us, we make sure to lock our cars and the doors to our homes every night, but we do not take the same advice for our devices. This book aims to provide you with tools and tactics to protect not only your devices but you, your family and your business from unwanted social engineering attacks. Although this book will discuss many technical concepts, we have specifically designed the book for everyone to read, from school kids to senior citizens. Cybercrime does not discriminate, be warned that anyone is fair game.

As you prepare to read or listen to each chapter, we will reference many websites.  We list all the sites at the end of each chapter. Besides each website, the reference will be a number in parentheses. At the end of the chapter, you will see a big "X" image.  Just look under this section for the website references.

Let's begin our journey,
Henry & Jimmy

# ACKNOWLEDGEMENTS

While writing this book, we received a great deal of support from our family and friends. Thank you to all the Social Engineers that share and make our world a better place. You know who you are!

We want to take a moment and humbly say **"THANK YOU"** for all of your support, encouragement, and feedback.

We also want to thank you, the reader or listener, for buying this book. Seriously, thanks a lot. The stuff in this book is important. Some of it will be tough, but it will make a big difference in your life and for the people you care about. Thanks to DEFCON Goons, Jeff Moss, & Social Engineering Community Village! I, Henry D, am proud to be an NFO Goon and part of the DEFCON family!

# Chapter 1

# COVID UNWIND AND CYBER THREATS

Beginning in early 2020, the world as we know it was transformed by the pandemic. In 2020, America went through the impeachment trial of a president, COVID-19, civil unrest, in-place shelters, working from home, layoffs, massive unemployment, disinformation campaigns, Zoom Bombings, and a presidential election, to name a few. As 2021 began, we watched the unthinkable, an attack on the U.S. capital. Many people realized remote work was here to stay, families transformed spare bedrooms into office or study spaces for kids, and the world continued to adjust to the changes from the COVID pandemic.

As we began 2022, remote work and distance learning became the new norms for many. Multiple surveys indicated that most employees did not want to return to a physical office. By spring 2022, many companies announced a return back to offices with the ability to have a hybrid work schedule. Employees had to be in the office some of the time, and the rest, they could work remotely.

Other companies said we are done with a physical office and will be a 100% remote organization. As the transformation continues, the need to be aware of digital defense and social engineering is imperative as the relationship and risks between remote work and home coexist.

The Federal Government's Cybersecurity and Infrastructure Agency's (CISA) website https://www.cisa.gov/sites/default/files/publications/Cybersecurity Awareness Month 2021 - Why is Cybersecurity Important.pdf (1) points out, "Did you know 43% of cyber-attacks target small businesses, and they have grown 400 percent since the outbreak began" During chaos and uncertainty, social engineers will take advantage of the worry and fear that is paralyzing our world. Now more than ever, it is important to safeguard yourself, your family, and your business associates. This chapter will take a look at some of the scams that happened between

2020-2022, while we wrote this book. As you go through the chapter, make sure to have an internet browser open. Throughout this book, we will highlight and showcase different stories. Cybercrime is everywhere, and almost every segment of modern society has been targeted. The following examples show just how common cybercrime is. Everything is hackable.

- **Seeing is Believing during the COVID-19 Pandemic:** Sometimes, it is really hard to believe that data is being hacked and sold, and that our economy and democracy are under attack. Over the last decade, many household names have been targeted. Information is Beautiful is a great website that can visualize data for you on various topics https://informationisbeautiful.net/visualizations/worlds-biggest-data-breaches-hacks/ (2). We decided to look up the world's biggest data breaches. It is a pretty shocking image. During COVID-19, we have seen cyber attack after cyber attack. Some of the most notable attacks were FireEye and Solar Winds.

- **Even Cyber Companies are Getting Attacked:** FireEye supports security teams with solutions that help mitigate threats. They are a leading provider and leader in cybersecurity across the globe. A group of state-sponsored hackers penetrated their network and stole tools. Take a few minutes and read the press release on this attack and the industry article https://www.fireeye.com/blog/products-and-services/2020/12/fireeye-shares-details-of-recent-cyber-attack-actions-to-protect-community.html and https://www.csoonline.com/article/3600893/fireeye-breach-explained-how-worried-should-you-be.html (3).

SolarWinds is an IT Management Software & Remote Monitoring company. The SolarWinds attack devastated many companies that used their services. In this attack, approximately 18,000 customers were infected by malware through a software update.  A joint statement from the FBI and NSA indicates that the attack was from Russia.  Take a few minutes to read further in this article https://www.cnet.com/news/fbi-nsa-and-cisa-say-solarwinds-hack-was-likely-of-russian-origin/  (4).

The bottom line is that cybercriminals are real. From the FireEye attack to all the companies listed on the Information is Beautiful website, cyber attacks do not discriminate.  As you read through the rest of this chapter, please take time to look at the links. The main goal is to support our claim that you need to learn how to protect yourself, your family, and your business from social engineering.

Ransomware has resurged in large numbers; the attacks are heavily focused on healthcare, local government, education, and private sectors.  Before we go further, let's take a quick second to explain what ransomware is in everyday person language.  Ransomware is software that will prevent your computer systems from working. Once on your system, you will get a message from someone that you have to pay money to get control back of your computer. According to the FBI's Internet Crime Complaint Center (IC3), "In 2021, the IC3 received 3,729 complaints identified as ransomware with adjusted losses of more than $49.2 million" https://www.ic3.gov/Media/PDF/AnnualReport/2021_IC3Report.pdf (5).  Let's take a quick look at some of the ransomware attacks.

- **Hospitals:** Cybercriminals are targeting hospitals in America.  For example, Becker's Hospital CFO report states that the Scripps Health attack in May of  2021 cost them $112 million https://www.beckershospitalreview.com/finance/scripps-records-q3-operating-loss-notes-cyberattack-cost-of-112-7m.html (6) & https://emma.msrb.org/

<u>P11517631-P11174379-.pdf</u> (7). Take a few minutes to read this informative article from Reuters that give you further insight into ransomware and hospitals <u>https://www.reuters.com/article/us-usa-healthcare-cyber/building-wave-of-ransomware-attacks-strike-u-s-hospitals-idUSKBN27D35U</u>  (8).

- **Local Government:** In 2019, a ransomware attack on Baltimore cost the city more than $18 million in damages and remediation. According to a TechRepublic article in August of 2020, "Municipal governments were subject to 45% of ransomware attacks in the past 12 months, and the other two sectors leading were healthcare with 22% and education with 15%. Corporations, which made up 27% of ransomware targets in the previous year, dropped to just 14% of targets. Logistics companies, which previously weren't a target, have started to be noticed as well, accounting for 5% of ransomware attacks in the past 12 months." <u>https://www.techrepublic.com/article/local-governments-continue-to-be-the-biggest-target-for-ransomware-attacks/</u> (9). Lastly, the EMSISOFT "State of Ransomware in the US: Report and Statistics 2021" shared that 77 state and city agencies and 1,043 schools were targeted by ransomware [https://blog.emsisoft.com/en/40813/the-state-of-ransomware-in-the-us-report-and-statistics-2021/](https://blog.emsisoft.com/en/40813/the-state-of-ransomware-in-the-us-report-and-statistics-2021/) (10).

- **Educational Institutions:** Educational Institutions, from Kindergarten to University, are now a large target. The State of K12 Cybersecurity report found that "During the calendar year 2020, the K-12 Cyber Incident Map cataloged 408 publicly-disclosed school incidents, including student and staff data breaches, ransomware and other malware outbreaks, phishing attacks and other social engineering scams, denial-of-service attacks, and a wide variety of other incidents. This is 18 percent more than were publicly disclosed during the prior calendar year (and—for the second year running—the most since the K-12 Cyber Incident Map first started tracking these incidents in 2016). This equates to more than two incidents per school day over the course of 2020." [https://k12cybersecure.com/wp-content/uploads/2021/03/StateofK12Cybersecurity-2020.pdf](https://k12cybersecure.com/wp-content/uploads/2021/03/StateofK12Cybersecurity-2020.pdf) (11). Later in the book, we share an example on an attack on an educational institution with the story of the Dark Overlord's attack on a school district.

- **Travel Services:** A company that does travel management paid $4.5M to hackers that stole information. Please take a few minutes to read the article from Reuters.  It delves into how they took an estimated 30,000 computers offline https://www.reuters.com/article/us-cyber-cwt-ransom/payment-sent-travel-giant-cwt-pays-4-5-million-ransom-to-cyber-criminals-idUSKCN24W25W (12).

Adversaries look at every possible angle to take advantage of an opportunity or situation. Let's now take a quick look at parts of our community that provide public safety and services for the citizen. According to the FBI's IC3 report, "phishing emails, remote desktop protocol exploitation, and exploitation of software vulnerabilities remain the top three initial infection vectors for ransomware incidents reported to the IC3." https://www.ic3.gov/Media/PDF/AnnualReport/2021_IC3Report.pdf  (5)

- **Ransomware Hack Puts Sensitive Azusa Police Department Documents Online:** International hackers use ransomware to exploit police and sell the data on the Dark Web https://www.latimes.com/california/story/2021-05-31/azusa-ransomware-hack-sensitive-police-documents-online (13). Nefarious threat actors shared

personally identifiable information data on the dark
web.  This can be catastrophic to those who are
affected.  An acquaintance of mine recently
experienced a ransomware attack. His only choices
were to either pay the ransom or have the data being
leveraged on him released to all his contacts.

- **Law Enforcement and Hackers:** During 2020, you
  may have heard about the term "Blue Leaks." Sensitive
  police records and files were leaked from all over the
  US by hackers on June 19, 2020, in response to
  George Floyd's death. https://krebsonsecurity.com/
  2020/06/blueleaks-exposes-files-from-hundreds-of-
  police-departments/ (14).

- **Cyber and Public Safety:** The American Military
  University published a safety guide for law
  enforcement, first responders, and firefighters.  https://
  www.iafc.org/topics-and-tools/resources/resource/
  protecting-against-cyberattacks (15) & https://
  www.iafc.org/docs/default-source/1comm-tech/
  protecting-against-cyberattacks-magazine_final.pdf?
  sfvrsn=584e810d_0 (16). Cybercriminals and social
  engineers will take advantage of proverbial "powder
  keg" situations.  What we mean by a powder keg is an
  event that occupies everyone's attention. Remember,
  as people are focused on one thing, this creates a

diversion for cybercriminals to attack a person or organization that is not in the spotlight. Years ago, I (Jimmy) had the opportunity to interview an engineer that would go to areas after a major storm to help restore power and assist with any other technical needs a community may have.  During the interview I was told that in these situations, hackers will take action while people's attention is diverted by a natural disaster. Also note that if you work in public safety, there are excellent resources provided through the Federal Government's Department of Homeland Security (DHS) Urban Area Security Initiatives (UASI). DHS gives funding to local UASIs to provide training to law enforcement and first responders https:// www.dhs.gov/science-and-technology/national-urban-security-technology-laboratory (17).

- **Cyber Threats and Supply Chains:** For lack of better words, the supply chain is how we get stuff from here to there. Just walk into your local grocery store or Costco. Everything in there comes from a supply chain. During COVID, there has been an increase in cyber attacks on the supply chain.  Throughout 2020, the FBI issued alerts of different attacks going after the supply chain, such as the Kwampirs Attack on healthcare organizations. Deloitte created an excellent briefing in

May of 2020 that looks at the rise of cyber attacks in supply chains during COVID. The report shared that 4 in 10 manufacturers had experienced a cyber incident in the last year https://www.helpnetsecurity.com/2020/11/03/disinformation-campaigns-social-media/ (18).

- **Cyber Fraud in Elections:** In my opinion (Jimmy), this past presidential election was one of the most polarizing elections our country has faced. Before the election, government organizations prepared for disinformation campaigns. In case you're wondering what a disinformation campaign is, it is an effort to assert false information through various mediums. In a recent conversation with an election expert, they told me that it doesn't matter whether the information is true or not; people will respond as if the information is true. Yikes! During the last presidential election in America, a Norton Life Lock study https://www.cisa.gov/sites/default/files/publications/PSA_voter_registration_data_508pobs.pdf (19) shows that 76% of Americans have, in fact, received disinformation firsthand. That means 3 out of 4 people you meet today have been targeted with disinformation. The study further went on to say that 58% feel disinformation can influence them.  If you are a betting social engineer, these are pretty good odds.

Humor us a few more minutes while we drill this point down a little further.  Let's say a disinformation campaign targets an extreme political group (you can pick which one) to believe that their opposition is violating their freedoms and needs to be stopped. Even if the opposing group did nothing, the other group will act as if it did.

Jimmy here; I remember one of the best disinformation campaigns that happened to me when I was in high school. I was hanging out with my boys, and the girl I was dating at the time walked up to us and ripped a note over my head and said a few explicative words and walked off. We did not have cell phones in the 80s, so the note was how we exchanged information. As I talked with my boys, I said, "Dude, I literally don't know what set her off." One of my good friends started laughing really hard as I was saying this.  He went on to tell me that he did not like the way this girl was treating me, so he wrote her a note, signed my name, and stuffed it in her locker.  From what I remember, the girl I had just begun dating was nice and did not know my friends or me too well.  She automatically assumed that I had written the note and reacted. Keep in mind that we were in high school.  The point here is that a simple note caused a disinformation campaign about high school Jimmy.  Jump ahead from the 80s to the present day.  Many people react to information without validating the source and that my friend is "so high school."

This last election really upset me with how my friends on social media responded to each other and reacted to disinformation campaigns. The FBI and the Cybersecurity Infrastructure and Security Agency (CISA) issued a public service announcement stating, "During the 2020 election season, foreign actors and cybercriminals are spreading false and inconsistent information through various online platforms in an attempt to manipulate public opinion, sow discord, discredit the electoral process, and undermine confidence in U.S. democratic institutions. These malicious actors could use these forums to also spread disinformation, suggesting successful cyber operations have compromised election infrastructure and facilitated the 'hacking' and 'leaking' of U.S. voter registration data. In reality, much U.S. voter information can be purchased or acquired through publicly available sources. While cyber actors have in recent years obtained voter registration information, the acquisition of this data did not impact the voting process or election results. In addition, the FBI and

CISA have no information suggesting any cyberattack on U.S. election infrastructure has prevented an election from occurring, prevented a registered voter from casting a ballot, compromised the accuracy of voter registration information, or compromised the integrity of any ballots cast." https://www.cisa.gov/sites/default/files/publications/PSA_voter_registration_data_508pobs.pdf (19).

In addition to disinformation campaigns, hackers will also target the election system. The Louisiana National Guard was called in to investigate cyberattacks targeting government organizations. https://www.reuters.com/article/us-usa-election-cyber-louisiana-exclusiv/exclusive-national-guard-called-in-to-thwart-cyberattack-in-louisiana-weeks-before-election-idUSKBN27823F (20). During the 2020 Black Hat conference, Matt Blaze from Georgetown University discussed "Stress Testing Democracy Election Integrity During A Global Pandemic" youtube.com/watch?v=IINittlfzGOtop (21).

Before we move on from election security, take five minutes to watch HBO's "Kill Chain: The Cyber War on America's Elections | Malware and Social Engineering" https://youtu.be/ArY_mFH_ZhA (22). Social engineering is defined as "The art of rolling victims into installing malicious software onto their own computer." The series goes on to say that the goal of social engineering is to lie or influence someone to simply gain trust.

I remember the fictional character Don Draper in "Mad Men" said it best. When you run into a problem with a campaign, the best move is to "change the conversation." Remember, people have, can, and will continue to harness disinformation and create a reaction by changing the proverbial conversation.  Whether the information is true or not has little bearing on how people react.

Our opinion is that people will react to the information at hand as if it is factual. Social engineers understand how to position information in a proverbial powder keg situation and get a rise or reaction out of someone. Sometimes that reaction is used as a distraction to conduct other nefarious activities or create physical friction in targeted cities.

## BE ON ALERT

During the pandemic, our society had a surge of attack vectors that spread throughout many facets that affected everyone. The following section will share with you places to go for information as well as samples of different cyber and social hacks.

- During COVID, many of us have lost our jobs and were actively seeking new employment. There were email scams circulating that offered people money. Beware of emails that offer you money.  This website shares a number of scam letters and what to be on the lookout for: http://www.sid.in-berlin.de/nedkelly-world/work%20at%20home%20scams%20II.html (23). My personal favorite is the letter from Mr. Bravo Ken and Kevin Godfrey.

FCC Chimes in too… Just in case the information we shared from the FTC was not convincing enough :), take a look at the Federal Communications Commission's (FCC) list of customer Scams from early on in the pandemic on the next page.

# COVID-19 Consumer Scams

As the COVID-19 pandemic continues, identity thieves and imposter scammers use text messages and robocalls to prey on consumers' virus-related fears.

- Scammers are still trying to swindle consumers or steal valuable personal or financial information through vaccine scams. Get tips to avoid these scams.
- COVID-19 text scams may falsely advertise a cure or offer bogus tests. Learn more and see examples of scam texts.
- Robocall scams have focused on health and financial concerns connected to COVID-19. Learn more and listen to actual scam audio.
- With the increase in online shopping, delivery notification scam calls and texts are also on the rise. Find out what to watch out for.
- Fraudsters are trying steal insurance information, money or both. Get tips to avoid offers for bogus COVID-19 antibodies tests or pharmacy scams.
- Contact tracing has become another ploy used by scammers. Learn about the tell-tale signs of a scam.
- Coronavirus scammers are targeting older Americans. Get information to share with seniors and their families.
- Peer-to-peer (P2P) mobile payment apps help consumers avoid contact with vendors, but missteps in P2P app use can be costly. Find out what you can do to avoid being scammed.

**Tips for Avoiding COVID-19 Scams**

- Do not respond to calls or texts from unknown numbers, or any others that appear suspicious.
- Never share your personal or financial information via email, text messages, or over the phone.
- Be cautious if you're being pressured to share any information or make a payment immediately.
- Scammers often spoof phone numbers to trick you into answering or responding. Remember that government agencies will never call you to ask for personal information or money.
- Do not click any links in a text message. If a friend sends you a text with a suspicious link that seems out of character, call them to make sure they weren't hacked.
- Always check on a charity (for example, by calling or looking at its actual website) before donating. (Learn more about charity scams.)

If you think you've been a victim of a coronavirus scam, contact law enforcement immediately. File coronavirus scam complaints online with the Federal Trade Commission.

For more information about scam calls and texts, visit the FCC Consumer Help Center and the FCC Scam Glossary.

The FCC has continued to process informal consumer complaints throughout the pandemic. View data, by category, for informal consumer complaints related to COVID-19 and the Keep Americans Connected Pledge. Learn more about the FCC response to the pandemic at fcc.gov/coronavirus.

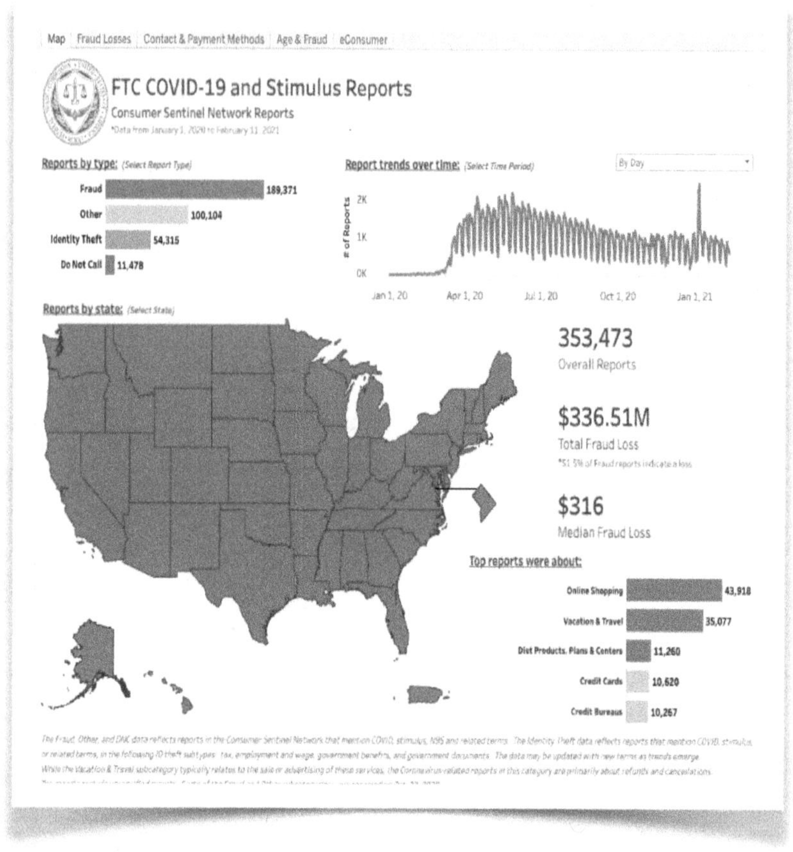



Jump ahead to 2022; the site gives great information on avoiding scams. Grab a browser and head out to https://www.fcc.gov/covid-scams (24).

- **World Health Organization (WHO):** Hackers have capitalized on COVID. In March of 2020, a hack was attempted on the WHO https://www.reuters.com/article/

us-health-coronavirus-who-hack-exclusive/exclusive-elite-hackers-target-who-as-coronavirus-cyberattacks-spike-idUSKBN21A3BN (25). WHO's Chief Information Security Officer said that they have seen a two-fold increase in attacks during the coronavirus.

■ **Spread Sheets and Contact Tracers:** Hackers never waste a pandemic. One of the most notable scams used spreadsheets and contact tracers to deceive. Imagine, in the early part of the pandemic, you get an email from a credible source with a spreadsheet attached saying it will provide an update on virus cases. This, in fact, happened. An email from John Hopkins came to people with a spreadsheet attachment. When the spreadsheet was opened, it downloaded a remote support tool opening the door for the victim to be hacked https://www.wired.com/story/covid-19-phishing-excel-ios-14-data-breaches/ (26).

The Bureau of Labor and Statistics' estimates around ten million people were unemployed during COVID. Numbers vary depending on where you look. During the pandemic, hackers took advantage of people who lost their jobs. There were scams where a person received an email from the company that laid them off. The email tells them they need to click on a website immediately for important information.

We are not sure how many of you have been laid off before, but let us assure it is a very scary feeling. For most of us, our first concern is finding a new job and filing for unemployment or any other benefits we can.  Being scammed is not usually at the forefront of your mind.

The Detroit Free Press published an excellent article entitled "Scammers tell people they're fired or may have COVID-19" https://www.freep.com/story/money/2020/08/12/scammers-fake-contact-tracing-termination-notice/5557821002/ (27). Pay attention to how they play to the fear most of us have about the ability to take care of ourselves and lose our jobs. For most Americans, it is our only source of revenue.  You may remember learning about Maslow's hierarchy of needs in high school or college, which focuses on personal motivation.  One of the core needs on Maslow's pyramid is safety.

Before we move off spreadsheets and contact tracers, there is one other healthcare scam worth mentioning.  During the early part of COVID in the spring of 2020, there was a website pretending to be a live map of the John Hopkins University tracking the Corona Virus https://www.forbes.com/sites/jessedamiani/2020/03/26/google-data-reveals-350-surge-in-phishing-websites-during-coronavirus-pandemic/?

sh=126de5fa19d5 (28).  During this season, Google data revealed that there was a 350% increase in phishing websites.

We began writing this book in early 2020, at the beginning of the pandemic.  At that time we could not have imagined the pandemic would last as long as it has.  In May of 2020, CSOonline.com published an article, "8 Ways attackers are exploiting the COVID-19 crisis" https://www.csoonline.com/article/3532825/6-ways-attackers-are-exploiting-the-covid-19-crisis.html (29).  Phishing emails are at the top of the list in this article.  In 2021 the FBI published the IC3 report. In 2021, the FBI received 3,279 complaints for Ransomware, with recorded losses estimated at $49.2 million https://www.ic3.gov/Media/PDF/AnnualReport/2021_IC3Report.pdf  (30).

In February of 2022, Proofpoint released its annual "State of the Phish" report https://www.proofpoint.com/us/newsroom/press-releases/proofpoints-2022-state-phish-report-reveals-email-based-attacks-dominated (31). The report, based on responses from 600 plus information technology and security professionals and 3,500 workers globally, revealed that phishing attacks are on the rise, and 83% of the respondents had one major phishing attack. The bottom line is that phishing worked at the beginning of the pandemic and is still a very powerful technique to attack an individual or their organization.

The world is continuously evolving.  The pandemic gave many of us a chance to reset while others struggled with isolation. We witnessed how great technology was in taking millions of people from office buildings and schools and transitioning them technologically to their homes. We captured in this first chapter how both technology and humans were exploited in the early stages of the COVID-19 pandemic. In the next chapter, we will provide you feedback on why you need to pay attention to social engineering. Try this free exercise & practice your phishing skills here: https:// what-is-phishing.cacyber.net/ or take this Google phish quiz! https://phishingquiz.withgoogle.com

## Website References

We realize there are many ways and styles to cite web references.  This book was written over a period of multiple years.  Please note that we don't have control if the content and links change over time.

(1)https://www.cisa.gov/sites/default/files/publications/
Cybersecurity Awareness Month 2021 - Why is
Cybersecurity Important.pdf
(2)https://informationisbeautiful.net/visualizations/worlds-
biggest-data-breaches-hacks/
(3)https://www.fireeye.com/blog/products-and-services/
2020/12/fireeye-shares-details-of-recent-cyber-attack-
actions-to-protect-community.html and https://
www.csoonline.com/article/3600893/fireeye-breach-
explained-how-worried-should-you-be.html
(4) https://www.cnet.com/news/fbi-nsa-and-cisa-say-
solarwinds-hack-was-likely-of-russian-origin/
(5)https://www.ic3.gov/Media/PDF/AnnualReport/
2021_IC3Report.pdf

(6)https://www.beckershospitalreview.com/finance/scripps-records-q3-operating-loss-notes-cyberattack-cost-of-112-7m.html

(7)https://emma.msrb.org/P11517631-P11174379-.pdf

(8)https://www.reuters.com/article/us-usa-healthcare-cyber/building-wave-of-ransomware-attacks-strike-u-s-hospitals-idUSKBN27D35U

(9)https://www.techrepublic.com/article/local-governments-continue-to-be-the-biggest-target-for-ransomware-attacks/

(10)https://blog.emsisoft.com/en/40813/the-state-of-ransomware-in-the-us-report-and-statistics-2021/

(11) https://k12cybersecure.com/wp-content/uploads/2021/03/StateofK12Cybersecurity-2020.pdf

(12) https://www.reuters.com/article/us-cyber-cwt-ransom/payment-sent-travel-giant-cwt-pays-4-5-million-ransom-to-cyber-criminals-idUSKCN24W25W

(13) https://www.latimes.com/california/story/2021-05-31/azusa-ransomware-hack-sensitive-police-documents-online

(14) https://krebsonsecurity.com/2020/06/blueleaks-exposes-files-from-hundreds-of-police-departments/

(15) https://www.iafc.org/topics-and-tools/resources/resource/protecting-against-cyberattacks

(16) https://www.iafc.org/docs/default-source/1comm-tech/protecting-against-cyberattacks-magazine_final.pdf?sfvrsn=584e810d_0

(17) https://www.dhs.gov/science-and-technology/national-urban-security-technology-laboratory

(18) https://www.helpnetsecurity.com/2020/11/03/disinformation-campaigns-social-media/

(19) https://www.cisa.gov/sites/default/files/publications/PSA_voter_registration_data_508pobs.pdf

(20) https://www.reuters.com/article/us-usa-election-cyber-louisiana-exclusiv/exclusive-national-guard-called-in-to-thwart-cyberattack-in-louisiana-weeks-before-election-idUSKBN27823F

(21) https://youtube.com/watch?v=llNittlfzG0top

(22) https://youtu.be/ArY_mFH_ZhA

(23) http://www.sid.in-berlin.de/nedkelly-world/work%20at%20home%20scams%20II.html

(24) https://www.fcc.gov/covid-scams

(25) https://www.reuters.com/article/us-health-coronavirus-who-hack-exclusive/exclusive-elite-hackers-target-who-as-coronavirus-cyberattacks-spike-idUSKBN21A3BN

(26) https://www.wired.com/story/covid-19-phishing-excel-ios-14-data-breaches/

(27) https://www.freep.com/story/money/2020/08/12/
scammers-fake-contact-tracing-termination-notice/
5557821002/

(28) https://www.forbes.com/sites/jessedamiani/2020/03/26/
google-data-reveals-350-surge-in-phishing-websites-
during-coronavirus-pandemic/?sh=126de5fa19d5

(29) https://www.csoonline.com/article/3532825/6-ways-
attackers-are-exploiting-the-covid-19-crisis.html

(30) https://www.ic3.gov/Media/PDF/AnnualReport/
2021_IC3Report.pdf

(31) https://www.proofpoint.com/us/newsroom/press-
releases/proofpoints-2022-state-phish-report-reveals-
email-based-attacks-dominated

(32) https://what-is-phishing.cacyber.net/

(33) https://phishingquiz.withgoogle.com

# NOTES

# Chapter 2
## SOCIAL ENGINEERING, WHY SHOULD I CARE?

Let's now talk about what social engineering is and why you should care. Knowledge of social engineering and the psychology of human behavior are components that can help you understand these types of threats. These threats are psychological and undermine weaknesses in humans.

My (Henry) life has always included a small portion of social engineering, by trying to see what I could get away with or performing as someone else. When I was in my twenties, I convinced a record store to give me a job through the use of social engineering.  The social engineering component and pretext include me disguising myself as someone from London, including the accent.

Now for the full story. I was dared by a friend to see if I could get hired by faking a British accent, and for some reason, it worked! I was hired and continued this fake identity for two months. Eventually I decided to tell the manager that I was really just a kid from the Bay Area who took a dare too far. As you can imagine, she was not happy. However, the interesting part was that she kept me as an employee because I was great with people and good at my job.

Another example of social engineering occurred at a large technology company in Silicon Valley. I did some pretexting and prep work before I tried to implement my attack. I was invited to a meeting at this large technology giant and thought, let me see how far I can get access to places I should not be. I knew some of the people at the company I was meeting with, what kind of cars they drove, as well as what they looked like. With this information in hand, I waited outside the company entrance from a close distance. This would allow me to see someone and identify them in their car. I watched and waited until I finally spotted someone I knew. Once they passed the parking security booth and parked their vehicle, I came in right after them. I was on the list for the meeting, so I was allowed to park.

I wore a hat and shirt with their company logo, and I had a fake badge I created using my computer and a printer. The next step was critical in my pretext. I hollered and waved to the person I knew before they entered the next building to access the rest of the authorized company building. This was critical, as the person checking company badges saw I knew a familiar employee. It was a small room with an attendant who checked company badges before you could proceed to the actual building.

My next step was smooth; the security attendant must have seen my company logo hat and shirt and that I knew someone in the company. I walked in, said hello, and they said good morning and told me to have a nice day. I was supposed to get a guest pass and be escorted to my meeting, but instead, I was able to socially engineer my way in as an employee (assumed). I was thrilled it worked!

My next challenge was to **tailgate** (walk in the building as someone else walks out, not needing a security badge to swipe to gain access. It almost worked; however, the employee I tried to walk in after said I need to see your security badge.

**OOH, I was Caught!** I told her my story about how I was here for a meeting but wanted to see how far I could get without proper security clearance. She was dumbfounded! We walked back, and the security guard gave a professional talking to me. Ultimately I was given my visitor badge and escorted to the meeting.

This is the largest social engineering hack I have attempted. I did it to see how far I could go, not to do harm. My intentions were to go back and tell the security guard to tighten up their security protocols. Disclaimer- Please do not attempt the actions described; it is irresponsible to attempt such without proper permission. The authors and publisher specifically disclaim any liability incurred from the use or application of the contents of this book. We will not be liable for others' actions; please do not attempt any of the social engineering examples in this book.

Quick vocabulary lesson- What are the five types of **phishing?** Phishing is sending emails or using other methods to get information from a target.

1. **Spear Phishing** targets a specific group or type of user, such as a system administrator.
2. **Whaling** attacks that target, a CEO, CFO, CISO, and CTO.
3. **Vishing** has the same intention as phishing but uses a voice call for the attack.

4. **Email Phishing** is the most popular and successful. They use email links to trick you, or language to get you to perform an action.

5. **Pharming,** leveraging the words "phishing" and "farming," is an online scam similar to phishing, where a website's traffic is manipulated, and confidential information is stolen https://www.cybertalk.org/pharming-vs-phishing/ (23) & https://youtu.be/mhNaqVF07Pw (24).

Let's now talk about what social engineering is and why you should care. Your call to action is to be aware of other people and your surroundings at all times. Whether you are in person, online, or on a mobile call out in public, there is a possibility of you being manipulated.

Let's revisit and define what social engineering is. Think of social engineering as the ability to hack or manipulate a person using things in their environment. George Washington University published an interview with Rachel Tobac in the fall of 2019 entitled "Human Hacker Playbook: How to Stop Me from Getting Your Personal Information" https://gwtoday.gwu.edu/human-hacker-playbook-how-stop-me-getting-your-personal-information (1). During the interview, Tobac said, "Most people think hackers need advanced technical skills or have to contact their targets

44

through fraudulent calls or emails to obtain personal and confidential information, but a growing number of them are actually getting sensitive information through companies' over-the-phone customer service."

Rachel Tobac is a really big deal in the world of social engineering. She is the CEO of Social Proof and is considered one of the world's foremost experts in social engineering. Tobac says, "Be politely paranoid. Social engineers will use publicly available pieces of information to build rapport with targets and gain their trust. Don't let someone authenticate with you using pieces of information that can be found online like your hobbies, coworkers' names, travel destinations, etc." https://www.synopsys.com/blogs/software-security/rachel-tobac-social-engineering-attacks-polite-paranoia/ (2), https://www.youtube.com/watch?v=hhHhOoecgvg&feature=youtu.be (3), https://www.hackerone.com/blog/Hacker-QA-Rachel-Tobac-Hacking-Companies-Through-Their-People (4).

It's worth watching Rachel Tobac's live demonstration where she hacks someone from CNN. We watched in person at (DEFCON), and it blew us away. Please take a few minutes to watch the linked video as she steals the interviewer's hotel points and moves his seat on an airplane flight live!

The point is that a social engineer can be anybody, anytime, anywhere https://www.facebook.com/cnn/videos/2424216847867646/ (5).

Throughout the year, we speak to many groups about social engineering. One of the first questions we ask folks is, **"What is Social Engineering?"** Once we get a few answers on social engineering, the next question is

**"Why should I care?"**

Not everyone is trustworthy, and in the cybersecurity world around us, we all need to be careful of whom we engage and what information we share. In the first chapter, we did a data dump describing many scenarios and examples of what has been taking place in our world. We want to emphasize the importance of how social engineering is used and how the everyday person can stop and consider the consequences before you click or engage with someone.

In chapter one, we shared with you example upon example of breaches that have recently happened. Now the question to ask is, what does this mean to me, and why should I care?

Everyone is at risk. You need to be able to identify when a scam is heading your way. Whether it is an email attack, voice email, or text, artificially intelligent machines you leave on in the home, or your car's infotainment systems, all these systems have vulnerabilities.

Have you enjoyed all the amazing things tech can offer? Want to stop the fear of being compromised or hacked? We wrote this book to help regular, everyday people. Most of the information out there is technical and lacks clear tactical steps.

If you were walking down the street in a dark alley and noticed someone following you, what would you do? Most people would look to remove themselves from potential harm and seek a safe place to go or run. The same is true with your mobile phone, laptop, smart appliances, and tablet.

Everyone needs general training and instruction. For example, you just wouldn't give a teenager the keys to a car before they've had driver's education. Well, the same is true for all the technology we have. From young children to your grandma, everyone is using technology. If you don't believe me, the next time you are in a store, check out all the babies glued to their parent's tablet or phone, watching a video while they shop. In the modern world, one is literally integrated into using tech at a very young age.

When we were growing up back in the 70s and 80s, there were a lot of scared straight commercials and shows. The idea was to show a kid the worst thing that can happen to them if they choose to go down a certain path. Now we are not here to endorse or support this program. We just want to make the point that you all reading this book really need to be "Scared Safe."

For all you parents or anyone who works with kids, we will share how people access kids online later in the book. Many parents have not been informed on how to protect their kids in the digital age. Later, we will share with you step-by-step, easy ways to help keep you, your business, and your family safe from cybercriminals and social engineers.

There is one thing all social engineers and cybercriminals have in common. **THEY DON'T DISCRIMINATE.** Whether you are famous or just a regular everyday person, you and your data are at risk. Your personal identification information (PII) is valuable to someone. Be very careful how much of your personal life you share with "big tech," as well as other organizations that want your data. The next time people ask for very personal information, just ask them to explain to you how their data is safe and what is to stop a hacker from accessing your Personally Identifiable Information, or (PII).

**Why Should you Care?**

Let's begin with the earlier question what is social engineering? For lack of better words, it is when a person can manipulate another person to gain access to information that they really have no business having. You might be thinking that sounds like a conman or hustler.

You are right; it is essentially a person misrepresenting themselves to get information from another person. Once they get this data, it will be used to access an individual's private information electronically through a computer or smartphone. People are literally hacking other humans just by talking to or manipulating their actions directly.

Before we give you some examples of social engineering, let's look at a few more definitions from reliable sources.

A Social Engineer comes from a term that Kevin Mitnick made popular in his book "The Art of Deception." In his book, he states that "the definition of social engineering in IT security is an attack which needs human interaction and manipulation in order to succeed in accessing network locations, confidential information, etc." https://www.amazon.com/Art-Deception-Controlling-Element-Security/dp/076454280X (6).

Department of Homeland Security defines social engineering attack as the following: "In a social engineering attack, an attacker uses human interaction (social skills) to obtain or compromise information about an organization or its computer systems. An attacker may seem unassuming and respectable, possibly claiming to be a new employee, repair person, or researcher and even offering credentials to support that identity. However, by asking questions, he or she may be able to piece together enough information to infiltrate an organization's network. If an attacker is not able to gather enough information from one source, he or she may contact another source within the same organization and rely on the information from the first source to add to his or her credibility." https://www.us-cert.gov/ncas/tips/ST04-014 (7).

According to Wikipedia, Social engineering is the psychological manipulation of people into performing actions or divulging confidential information https://en.wikipedia.org/wiki/Social_engineering_(security) (8). For us, a simple term is a person that can manipulate others to do things and access information.

At this point, you may be starting to see how social engineering works. Just in case you need a little more convincing, take a quick look at the FBI's 2020 IC3 report. IC3 stands for the Internet Crime Complaint Center. According to the report, "IC3 received a record number of complaints from the American public in 2020: 791,790, with reported losses exceeding $4.1 billion." https://www.ic3.gov/Media/PDF/AnnualReport/2020_IC3Report.pdf (9).

Social engineering is an effective and dangerous weapon. Here are statistics worth considering. https://purplesec.us/resources/cyber-security-statistics/ (10), https://www.embroker.com/blog/cyber-attack-statistics/ (11), https://securityintelligence.com/articles/most-digital-attacks-today-involve-social-engineering/ (12):

✓ 98% of cyber attacks rely on social engineering.

✓ 43% of the IT professionals said they had been targeted by social engineering schemes in the last year.

✓ New employees are the most susceptible to socially engineered attacks, with 60% of IT professionals citing recent hires as being at high risk.

✓ 21% of current or former employees use social engineering to gain a financial advantage, for revenge, out of curiosity, or for fun.

✓ Social engineering attempts spiked more than 500% from the first to the second quarter of 2018.

✓ The number of breach incidents by type:

- Identity theft – 65%

- Account access – 17%

- Financial access – 13%

- Nuisance – 4%

- Existential data – 1%

The FBI found that digital crime complaints increased by about 70% between 2019 and 2020. Many of those complaints involved some form of social engineering https://securityintelligence.com/articles/4-social-engineering-threats-to-keep-an-eye-on-and-how-to-stop-them/ (13). Phishing attacks, non-payment or non-delivery ploys, and extortion scams were the most prevalent types of ruses, with romance and confidence schemes, investment fraud attempts, and business email compromise (BEC) campaigns costing their victims the most. The last method of attack accounted for $1.8 billion throughout 2020, according to the IC3. https://www.ic3.gov/Media/PDF/AnnualReport/ 2020_IC3Report.pdf  (14).

Criminals will target everyone, everyday and anywhere. Their scams can affect every aspect of our lives. We talked about this in detail in chapter one. We want to share with you some more examples and articles on how serious cybercrime and social engineering scams are around the world.


- It can happen to you! Barbara Corcoran, from Shark Tank, lost $400K to a business email compromise. This is the reality of social engineering. https:// www.proofpoint.com/us/corporate-blog/post/shark-tanks- barbara-corcoran-loses-nearly-400k-bec-attack-what-you- need-know  (15).
- Disney is Getting Hacked. In 2019 Disney Plus accounts were hacked, and it was not a good thing! This article shares a story of an account member and their trials and tribulations with this attack and their use of Open Source Intelligence (OSINT).  https://securityboulevard.com/ 2020/03/was-your-new-disney-plus-account-stolen/  (16).

One of the biggest questions we have considered while writing this book is how people fall prey and simply miss seeing the scam. If you get a chance, read Malcolm Gladwell's book "Talking to Strangers. In this book, Gladwell shows how people literally miss the intentions and context of another person while communicating. Please take a few minutes to listen to Gladwell on why detecting liars based on behavior is so tricky. https://www.cbc.ca/news/canada/malcolm-gladwell-interview-1.5303203 (17).

Another interesting article in the Harvard Business Review states that a study found "people can correctly identify whether someone is telling a lie only 54% of the time, not much better odds than a coin flip." The article goes on to say that we are "wired to readily accept information that conforms to our preexisting assumptions or hopes." https://hbr.org/2016/07/how-to-negotiate-with-a-liar?cm_sp=Article-_-Links-_-Comment (18).

Social engineers understand how to connect and build rapport quickly and with anyone. Robin Dreeke is a best-selling author and retired FBI Chief of the Counterintelligence Behavioral Analysis Program. In his book, "It's Not All About Me: The Top Ten Techniques for

Building Quick Rapport with Anyone," https://
www.amazon.com/Its-Not-All-About-Techniques-ebook/dp/
B0060YIBLK (19) he delves into ten strategies to help you
connect and build rapport. If social engineers understand
how to do this, you should be aware too. We encourage you
to read the book. We came across another blog from
Farnam Street that talks about negotiating with a liar that
highlights the ten techniques discussed in Dereeke's book.
https://fs.blog/2013/07/building-trust/   (20).


Before we head on to the next chapter and, I want to talk
about a famous psychology experiment that was done
decades before social media existed. Dr. Stanley Milgram,
Ph.D., conducted the small world experiment that looked at
how people are connected. In short, Milgram had 160
different people who lived in Omaha, Nebraska, all send a
letter to the same person in Sharon, Massachusetts. Now,
this is the super-interesting point; of the 160 letters, only 24
reached the person in Massachusetts. The experiment
revealed that 16 of the 24 letters were given to the person in
Massachusetts by the same person. The experiment showed
that the 64 letters reached the target through five to six
people.

The idea of people from another state being connected to a stranger by only five to six degrees of separation is mind-blowing. You may remember the game "Six Degrees of Kevin Bacon" people played. They looked at how they may be connected to Kevin Bacon. Bacon also turned the six-degrees game into a charity called sixdegrees.org to further connect people to causes.

So if an experiment before the time of Facebook, Twitter, TikTok, Instagram, and Linked In could connect people from one part of the country to another part with just six people, imagine how easy it is to connect and learn about people just by everything they put on social media. For the record, we love social media and all the great things one can do and connect to in the modern world. However, you need to be careful.

Just last night, I (Jimmy) watched a totally-crowdsourced TV series called the "Chosen" that people watch using an app. This is a faith-based series that connects people from all over the world. We truly are becoming more and more connected with the click of a mouse.

**The Social Media Experiment**

We love Jack Vale. Jack has taken his skills from

inconspicuously recording himself farting on unassuming victims in stores to social engineering people. Check out this video that will show you a social media experiment Jack did on unassuming people. https://www.facebook.com/officialjackvale/videos/social-media-experiment/2248514008796203/ (21) This should make you think twice about what you share with strangers. I know we have a ton of links in this book, but please watch this one, and then ask yourself what you tell and show the world about your private life, your family, work, kids, travel plans, pets, and opinions.

## The Cold A.I. (Just one more story before we wrap up chapter two)

Humor us while we give you one more example.  Many people have some kind of device on in their house that they leave on all day. Each of these devices comes with an artificial intelligence (A.I.) that you can ask questions to about the weather, sports scores, or anything you can imagine.

Have you ever been talking about something, and all of a sudden, an ad appears?  This is because your A.I. device is listening and most likely sharing your information. One of our acquaintances had an A.I. device that controlled everything in their house, from heating to lights.  This person lived in a really cold part of America that gets a ton of snow.  Our acquaintance went on a vacation to the beach for the week.  He set the temperature on his system to make sure the home would stay warm during their leave.  While the A.I. took over and decided that the house needed to conserve energy and turned down the temperature really low.  Now there was no human in the house for a week.  When our friend came home, his house was very cold which could damage several things in his home in this cold environment.  Needless to say, the A.I. was kindly asked to leave the home and not come back :).

The goal of this chapter was to answer the question why should you care about social engineering.  This chapter has 23 website references as well as our opinions on why you should care.  The bottom line is that hackers and social engineers care, and so should you.  In chapter three, we are going to get into how social engineering works.

**Website References**

We realize there are many ways and styles to cite web references.  This book was written over a period of multiple years.  Please note that we don't have control if the content and links change over time.

(1)https://gwtoday.gwu.edu/human-hacker-playbook-how-stop-me-getting-your-personal-information

(2)https://www.synopsys.com/blogs/software-security/rachel-tobac-social-engineering-attacks-polite-paranoia/

(3)https://www.youtube.com/watch?v=hhHhOoecgvg&feature=youtu.be

(4)https://www.hackerone.com/blog/Hacker-QA-Rachel-Tobac-Hacking-Companies-Through-Their-People

(5) https://www.facebook.com/cnn/videos/2424216847867646/

(6) https://www.amazon.com/Art-Deception-Controlling-Element-Security/dp/076454280X

(7) https://www.us-cert.gov/ncas/tips/ST04-014

(8) https://en.wikipedia.org/wiki/
Social_engineering_(security)

(9) https://www.ic3.gov/Media/PDF/AnnualReport/
2020_IC3Report.pdf

(10)    https://purplesec.us/resources/cyber-security-
statistics/

(11)    https://www.embroker.com/blog/cyber-attack-
statistics/

(12)    https://securityintelligence.com/articles/most-digital-
attacks-today-involve-social-engineering/

(13)    https://securityintelligence.com/articles/4-social-
engineering-threats-to-keep-an-eye-on-and-how-to-stop-
them/

(14)    https://www.ic3.gov/Media/PDF/AnnualReport/
2020_IC3Report.pdf

(15)    https://www.proofpoint.com/us/corporate-blog/post/
shark-tanks-barbara-corcoran-loses-nearly-400k-bec-
attack-what-you-need-know

(16)    https://securityboulevard.com/2020/03/was-your-new-
disney-plus-account-stolen/

(17)    https://www.cbc.ca/news/canada/malcolm-gladwell-
interview-1.5303203

(18)    https://hbr.org/2016/07/how-to-negotiate-with-a-liar?
cm_sp=Article-_-Links-_-Comment

(19)    https://www.amazon.com/Its-Not-All-About-
Techniques-ebook/dp/B0060YIBLK

(20) https://fs.blog/2013/07/building-trust/

(21) https://www.facebook.com/officialjackvale/videos/
social-media-experiment/2248514008796203/

(22) https://www.cybertalk.org/pharming-vs-phishing/.

(23) https://youtu.be/mhNaqVF07Pw

# NOTES

62

# Chapter 3

# HOW SOCIAL ENGINEERING WORKS

Let's take a quick break to recap what we have learned so far. In chapter one, we shared with you different cyber and social engineering scams. The point of chapter one was to make you aware that social engineering is something to take seriously. Next, chapter two discusses what social engineering is and why you should care. Chapter three will take you through how social engineering and cyber scams work.

To learn more about the use of persuasion that social engineers use, Robert Cialdini's book "Influence: The Psychology of Persuasion" discusses seven principles to demonstrate what we do when we make quick decisions. They are as follows: Reciprocity, Scarcity, Authority, Liking, Commitment, Consensus, and Unity. These are explained in detail at https://www.phishlabs.com/ blog/brain-hacking-social-engineering-effective/ (35).

As with chapters one and two, we have more links. Remember, this book is designed to share with you a concept and then have you review an example.



Humans are hacking other humans by talking to them, emailing and texting them, and tricking them into going to websites that get their private information. A social engineer can hack you for valuable information both online and in person.  In order to protect yourself from divulging sensitive information, we will teach you how social engineers use tactics to steal the proverbial keys to your castle. If you learn how to spot sketchy emails, online scams, and avoid someone stealing information from you in person, via the phone, online gaming, messaging apps, and on social sites, you may be able to get ahead of someone hacking you and have and possibly save yourself from future headaches and financial loss.

Social engineers will come at you from a variety of angles. Whatever the form and attack, rest assured they will use tactics like fear, urgency, disaster, and political unrest to push buttons. Over the last five years, I have watched social engineers do everything from stealing money from grieving widows to running scams on people laid off work due to COVID. They do this because they can make money from your information.

There is so much out there. We will show you common hacks and how to protect yourself if you are socially engineered. From a little kid to a middle-aged person to your grandma, social engineers do not discriminate, are watching, and will attack when you least expect it.

Before we start breaking down how social engineering works, take a few minutes and watch this video about how a woman uses the sound of a crying baby to access someone's information. https://www.youtube.com/watch?v=8rrpVtnV_wM  (2).

The goal of this chapter is to explain how social engineering works. We will look at how social engineers and cybercriminals prey on people's emotions, exploit situations, and create fake personas.

We first saw the live version of the video above at DEFCON a few years ago https://www.youtube.com/watch?v=8rrpVtnV_wM (2). The woman in the video, Jessica Clark, created a fictional scenario to trick a person from a phone company into giving her access to someone else's mobile phone account with the help of the sound of a baby crying.

Jessica called a cell phone provider stating that she and her fictional husband were applying for a loan. He was supposed to add her to the account on his cell phone. She has a prerecorded sound of a baby crying in the background as she is speaking.

Within the first few seconds of this call, she demonstrated to the person on the other end of the phone call that she was a busy mom with a new baby trying to help her family apply for a new loan. She also indicated to the person listening that her husband told her to get this done today. In under 30 seconds, she gained access to someone else account. The unsuspecting person on the other end of the phone probably felt good that they were helping this busy mom with a new baby, or the sound of the baby was overwhelming to them.

Just in case you need a little more convincing that social engineering is a real problem, let's look at the Target breach in 2013. If you are like me, Target is a store that you hit up pretty regularly. Six days before Christmas in 2013, Target issued a press release stating that "Approximately 40 million credit and debit card accounts may have been impacted between Nov. 27 and Dec. 15, 2013." https://corporate.target.com/press/releases/2013/12/target-confirms-unauthorized-access-to-payment-car (3). Forty million credit and debit cards, in my brain, this amounts to 40 million people. Forty million people is just about the number of people living in California. According to the 2020 Census, California has approximately 39,576,757 people living in the state. That is a lot of people. Gatefy, a Cybersecurity company, published an article citing that the attack came through a phishing email of a Target partner company. Through this email, hackers got access to one of the biggest department store chains in the USA. Once inside the network, the hackers accessed credit and debit card numbers. https://gatefy.com/blog/real-and-famous-cases-social-engineering-attacks/ (4).

The aftermath of these types of breaches is catastrophic! The Dark Web is where criminals and bad actors buy and sell data for nefarious uses. Once a breach happens, threat actors will expose Personal Identifiable Information (PII), for example, credit card numbers, social security numbers, and other confidential data. To date, you could buy a legitimate social security number on the Dark Web for under $10.

Please take a few minutes to read this article from Gatefy that talks about the Target data breach as well as other attacks over the last decade, like the TV show "Shark Tank," Toyota, government organizations, Sony Pictures, and the Democratic Party. An outside threat actor can trick someone into gaining access to information that can be sold for profit or harm an organization. https://gatefy.com/blog/real-and-famous-cases-social-engineering-attacks/ (4).

Let's now take a closer look at how people can leverage technology, sounds, visuals, and emotions to attack.

**7-38-55 Rule (Learn It and Know It)**

The video you just watched of Jessica Clark masterfully using sound and very few words showed how she was able to manipulate the customer service representative and to get what she wanted. Spend time carefully watching how people use sounds to persuade in your environment. Listen to people's tones and how they reflect or convey emotion.

7-38-55 has truly been one of the most powerful concepts we have learned. Jimmy was lucky enough to have a friend in the DC Metro area that trained politicians on how to speak and present. Knowing that Jimmy had studied speech communication and rhetoric in college, his friend said come and listen to my class. In this class, people were taught about the 7-38-55 principle.

Dr. Albert Mehrabian developed a theory that when we communicate with others, people respond to the following:

✓ 7% percent to the words we speak
✓ 38% percent to the sound of our voice
✓ 55% to body language.

Let this soak in for a few minutes. People respond more to sound and our body language and less to the words we use. In the video referenced earlier in the chapter, watch the words the woman uses versus the impact of the sound. Think about how you would respond if you were out in a store and saw and could hear a mom being upset with a small infant crying. What would your response be? For us, we would ask if we could help. It is just how we are wired.

**Environment**

Another powerful tool of the social engineer is your environment. During the season we were writing, the vibe in America was heavy. Over the last three years, we all have experienced:

- Watching the impeachment trials of President Trump, Capitol Storming, and the Election of President Biden
- Learning about COVID and watching large technocratic organizations used as communication mediums to censor free speech. Just so we are clear, we are not pro-elephant or pro-donkey. Our grandfathers fought in WW2, we read 1984 in 1984, and we get scared of any form of censorship. Just keep your eyes on any organizations that use social engineering tactics to drive policies and agendas.
- Understanding how to be safe from COVID
- Transitioning school and work to the home
- Waiting for our stimulus checks
- Unemployment
- Watching the news on spikes in the spread of the virus
- Deciding what is fake news/disinformation
- Worrying about jobs and layoffs. We know people that have been out of work for over a year.

· Seeing the death of George Floyd and, sadly, subsequent shootings of school children and people in subways and stores.

Our point here is that we all deal with many things in our environment. Many social engineers will create chaos during times of upheaval in our world. Many people that like to create division and distrust are known as trolls. All joking aside, there was a spoof about trolling the other day in a South Park episode where they show how a troll works and creates harm for the lives of people all over the world. Of course, it's South Park; viewers, beware.

Internet Trolls are people who want to provoke and upset others online for their own amusement. https://www.howtogeek.com/465416/what-is-an-internet-troll-and-how-to-handle-trolls/ (5) Troll farming, is a group of Internet trolls that seek to interfere with political and decision-making opinions. https://en.wikipedia.org/wiki/Troll_farm (6).

During the summer of 2020, there was a great deal of social media rhetoric for both black lives matter as well as blue lives matter. The Science Alert during this season posted an article that discussed troll farms attacking blue lives and black lives matter to create chaos. The article references a paper from the University of Washington that studied social movement communications and how they frame messaging, as well as what messaging is used to counter-frame. The paper points out that social media has been used to frame messaging.

Just to dig a little deeper on framing. There were many people we were connected to on social media that literally became unhinged before, during, and after the election. Whether you were for Trump or Biden, people were treating each other awful by angrily ranting to anyone that opposed their view. We deleted our accounts from one social platform because of how disturbed people were getting.

Reports are coming out all the time on the negative impact social media may have on health. https://www.sciencealert.com/fake-accounts-are-constantly-manipulating-what-you-see-on-social-media-here-s-how (7). Let's just think about it for a few minutes. With the pandemic, many people, had initially been locked away from family, friends, and coworkers for over a year. Today, stress is still high. There was massive framing going on everything from the election to COVID. I am betting that when scholars review the COVID period of the world, we will find that there were those that trolled on the fear of people during this time for nefarious purposes.

A social engineer understands how to get our attention in any environment. Maslow did a fascinating study on human behavior and demonstrated that people have the following needs:

1. Basic needs for food, water, and shelter
2. Being safe
3. Need for people, love, and relationships
4. Feeling accomplished
5. Self Fulfillment

As we look at the mental state of Americans right now, most of us are focused on one, two and three on the list above. Watching the news and hearing information about layoffs, the ongoing impact of COVID 19, and how one political party hates the other one, may keep us informed but chances are it also makes people feel fear and worry.

Let's say someone is watching your posts on Linked In, Twitter, Instagram, TikTok, and Facebook. In general, you have been pretty upset lately and have been posting things that show you are overall frustrated with the country and concerned for the well-being of your family.  Next, they look you up on LinkedIn and get an idea of where you work. After monitoring your company's status and hearing your organization is having issues, they decide that you are the perfect mark.

The social engineer sends you an email or maybe uses "snail mail" with a letter and envelope (that looks really official) saying that you will be furloughed and need to click on a link to be able to receive your COVID severance package.

The moment people hear that they will lose their jobs, they are flooded with emotions of fear, worry, and survival. At that moment, you only have one goal: to find another job to take care of yourself and your family. The needs Maslow mentioned on self-fulfillment and feeling accomplished go out the freaking window. It's survival! You need to get another job to get money to survive.

Most of us would click on the link to survive; who does not need a little hope in a dark time? Knowing this, the social engineer leverages your fear and creates a way for you to feel safer by clicking on the link. The ulterior motive of the social engineer and the email/letter may be to gain access to your organization's network and access valuable information they can monetize.

In April 2020, Information Security Magazine reported on a story where employees in Great Britain were being targeted by phishing scams pretending to be from Her Majesty's Revenue and Customs (HMRC).  According to the article, people were sent emails on how to access a relief fund. The BBC reported that 5-10% of the HMRC furlough cash had been wrongly awarded.

 Many times social engineers will make up a fictitious company or government agency and pose as an employee. Always verify when someone calls you, who they are and what they want, especially if they ask for money.

**Emotions and Fears**

There are many weapons in a social engineer's arsenal. Social engineers are very smart. One of the biggest areas they prey on, is our fears.  Go back through chapter one and look at many scams that took place during COVID. COVID made us all feel unsafe, scared, and unsure of the future of our health and many of our jobs. Be very careful when you get a message from someone you don't know saying that you have not done something and you have to take immediate action, or else there will be severe consequences.

The other area that social engineers prey on is loneliness or the need to feel loved.  We are always amazed at the many stories we hear of social engineers connecting with young girls and boys through a messaging app and developing a relationship.

Not long ago, we attended a human-trafficking training, where we heard several presentations from law enforcement as well as Opel Singleton from Millionkids.org. A story was told about how a sexual predator identified a young girl and developed a relationship with her online through a messaging app. Using a technique of asking the young girl questions and learning what she was frustrated with in life, the predator began to paint a picture of what life and a relationship would be like with him. This caused the young girl to meet the predator and ultimately get trafficked by him.  Spend some time looking through the National Center for Missing and Exploited Children at https://www.missingkids.org/ourwork/publications#exploited (8).

Later in the book, we will discuss a game plan to protect your kids online and teach the social-martial arts.

Parenting in the modern era of technology is hard, and kids hide things on different accounts; however, you need to make sure that strangers are not hunting your kids. It's better to have your kid safe and not like you.  This is one you can't stick your head in the sand on and say I don't understand tech.  You most likely pay for your child's device and internet connection.  Trust me; you will be doing them a favor.

***The point we are making here is that cyber criminals prey on emotions and seek those they can manipulate.***

There is story after story in the news about people from every walk of life that get hustled.   At the end of chapter two, we shared some insights on how people will lie and that you have to be careful when talking and communicating with strangers.  A Harvard Business Review stated that a study found that "people can correctly identify whether someone is telling a lie only 54% of the time not much better odds than a coin flip."  The article goes on to say that we are "wired to readily accept information that conforms to our preexisting assumptions or hopes." If you missed this link in the last chapter, please take a few minutes to read this article: https://hbr.org/2016/07/how-to-negotiate-with-a-liar?cm_sp=Article-_-Links-_-Comment (9).

The reason people send emails that prey on people's emotions is that they simply work. Earlier in the book, we discussed the FBI's internet crime report (IC3).  This is just one of the many kinds of scams people use to social engineer a stranger.

So by now, you have the idea that a stranger communicating with you online could be lying and may use emotion or a heated circumstance to get you to take action. The other thing to keep in mind is that person approaching you may not be who they say they are.  Did you know it is pretty easy to create fake IDs and photos?  Let's take a quick look at how someone can create a fake photo and ID.

**Fake Personas**

Many social engineers use fictional accounts and fake personas.  This is called a sock puppet. Here is another example of an email we received on September 5, 2020. Now we are not betting men, but we are pretty it is a safe bet that the email on the adjacent page is a scam, using a fake persona.

*"Dear Friend.*
*My name is Mr James Kumah. I write to seek your services in a private and confidential matter*
*regarding an unaccounted fund in our bank here in Ghana during the last two years 2018 end of the year's report. As a Regional Manager in this Bank, I deposited this fund in an ESCROW CALL ACCOUNT at our headquarters pending when I shall get a reliable person.*

*This requires a private arrangement. Could you perhaps be able to receive these funds under legal claims then I will file you in. I will appreciate for fewer questions asked and your participation will be 40% of the total money. There are practically no risks involved, the transaction will be executed under a legitimate arrangement that will protect you from any breach of the law, it will be simply a bank-to-bank transfer.*

*I have all the details and will file you in if you are really willing. Your major role would be to provide an existing account or open a new bank account where the funds   will be transferred and stand as the original depositor of this fund in our bank, as long as you will remain honest to me till the end for this important business trusting in you and believing that you will never let me down either now or in future.*

*Once this fund is transferred into your account, I shall resign from my job and bring my family to start a new life in your country. The funds in question are quite large, Twelve million five hundred thousand United States Dollars($12,500,000.00).*

*I will expect a straight answer from you. If yes, please get back to me so that we can work out the modalities without further delay. I will be monitoring the whole situation here in this bank until you confirm the money in your account and ask me to come down to your country for subsequent sharing of the fund according to percentages previously indicated and further investment, either in your country or any country you advice us to invest in. All other necessary vital information will be sent to you when I hear from you I look forward to receive your email.*

*Regards.*
*Mr James Kumah"*

Just in case Mr. Kumah was

not convincing enough,

here are some more texts I

have received over the last

year.  I am purposely leaving

out the websites

that were included in the

message because you should

not click on these links.

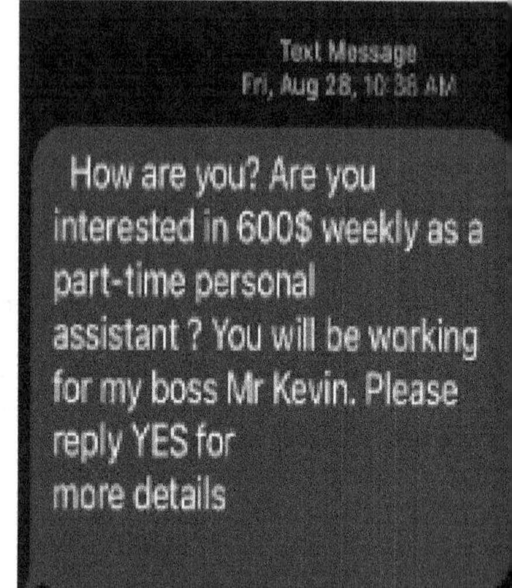


*"This is Ava Mae from Quick Lend and I have been permitted to offer you a potential pre approval for up to $1800.  Please complete your docs"*

*"This is from USPS (United States Postal Office) concerning a a schedule deliver. Read here (website link) Jimmy."* Not a great idea to send to Jimmy or Henry :) !!!

*"This Jane S from customer service and I have been authorized to offer you a potential pre approval for up to $2380. Please view your forms."* BTW much better deal than Ava Mae :).

**"This is yours, We found a refund payment of $681.25 is due to you on your insurance Policy. Claim REFUND HERE:"**

By the way, when a text like this comes, don't ever click on the links they give. Also, make sure to block the contact and delete messages from your phone. We have seen another technique where you are part of a group text message with 20-plus other people. Block everyone and all unknown messages and numbers. Remember that you can ignore texts, delete texts, and not answer any calls you are unfamiliar with.

Let's take a closer look at how social engineers really do this. Please open up a browser and take a look at these websites:

- ✓ So let's begin with a good photo. Take a quick look at https://thispersondoesnotexist.com/ (10). Hackers will use websites to create a fake persona for two reasons one is to protect the hacker's identity as well as have it be nontraceable. The tools are readily available and easy to navigate. The basic idea is to create a fake person the hacker will use to manipulate you.

- ✓ Next, let's figure out a name to go with that photo. The following website will let you come up with a name from anywhere in the world; please take a quick look at https://www.behindthename.com (36) and play around with a few names.

✓ Let's now get some fictional facts about this person. The first place to start is your gender, name, and where you are from. Head over to Fake Name Generator at https://www.fakenamegenerator.com/gen-random-us-us.php (37)

✓ You will probably need a fake email account. You can figure that one out yourself.  Just take a look in your search engine for temporary email accounts.

✓ Remember, a fake identity is random information put together to look like it is a real person, but everything is a lie. Before you move on to the next section of this chapter, open up a browser and visit https://www.elfqrin.com/fakeid.php (38)

This last section scares us but is riveting. There are sites where you can literally get an entirely fake social profile. Take a look at the next link, which is a story from Wired entitled "Meet Mia Ash, the Fake Woman Iranian Hackers Used to Lure Victims" https://www.wired.com/story/iran-hackers-social-engineering-mia-ash/ (11). The article goes on to tell us that Mia is 30 and works as a photographer. She has over 500 friends on Facebook and Linked In.  Mia is what you call a "digital honey trap."  She has a believable profile with a long history that makes you think this person is legit. But it is a lie. The point here is to be careful when you begin communicating with strangers on the internet.

**Sock Puppets** /fake identity- how they work: https://www.ehacking.net/2021/04/the-ultimate-sock-puppets-tutorial-for-osint-operators.html (12a).

## How Do Social Engineers Collect Data on You?

Our social profiles and the data we look up tell a great deal about us.  Steve Jobs once said, "I believe people are smart, and some people want to share more data than other people do. Ask them. Ask them every time. Make them tell you to stop asking them if they get tired of your asking them. Let them know precisely what you're going to do with their data." Watch this video (12) https://www.youtube.com/watch?v=3U8w58022TA on Alethe Denis, Social Engineer winner of Black Badge at DEFCON, describing how she confronted an Online Scammer.

Another newer tactic is MFA Fatigue. According to Bleeping Computer, "An MFA Fatigue attack is when a threat actor runs a script that attempts to log in with stolen credentials over and over, causing what feels like an endless stream of MFA push requests to be sent to the account's owner's mobile device."
https://www.bleepingcomputer.com/news/security/mfa-fatigue-hackers-new-favorite-tactic-in-high-profile-breaches/

(39) The goal is to keep this up, day and night, to break

down the target's cybersecurity posture and inflict a sense of "fatigue" regarding these MFA prompts.

Apple has an amazing website that is called "A Day in the Life of Your Data." People are tracked when they are online and offline. The Apple website referenced below states, "A complex ecosystem of websites, apps, social media companies, data brokers, and ad tech firms track users online and offline, harvesting their personal data. This data is pieced together, shared, aggregated, and used in real-time auctions, fueling a $227 billion-a-year industry." Take a pause reading the book and check out this site at: https://www.apple.com/privacy/docs/A_Day_in_the_Life_of_Your_Data.pdf (13).

Let's just take a few minutes and look at some social media platforms: Facebook, Instagram, LinkedIn, and Twitter.

**Facebook:** The average Facebook bio shares with people your posts. Post can tell people about your likes and dislikes, locations, and people you are connected to when you tag them in a picture. The about section can give information on:

1. Your job
2. What you look like

3. Where you went to high school and college

4. Your current city and hometown

5. Are you married, single, or in a relationship?

6. There is a section to tell people where you have lived in the past and how to get in contact with you directly.

7. There is another section on family relationships.

8. In the details about your section, one can share a summary, other nicknames they have, and favorite quotes.

9. There is another menu that shares your favorite videos, sports, music, movies, TV shows, Books, Likes, and groups you are in on Facebook.

10. Photos show people everything- where you live, your children, your significant others, where you vacation, where you shop, and who you are friends with on Facebook. We are always shocked when people announce to strangers when they are on vacation, where they are staying, and having drinks.  People who are under the influence of alcohol are much easier to manipulate if you are going to social engineer them in person. Watch Data Transparency "What every User Should Know About Facebook.":  https://www.youtube.com/watch?v=YgKz_KLE_yk&t=110son (14).  Facebook and Instagram allow you to download ALL your data; you will be surprised by what you see!

(15) How to access **Facebook** https://www.facebook.com/help/212802592074644 (16) **Instagram** https://help.instagram.com/contact/505535973176353!

Just take a pause and look at all the information that a hacker with a fake persona may access.  When we teach classes on this, we will pick a random persona on one of our Facebook profiles and talk about what we can learn about this person in 15 minutes.  You would be surprised.  Here is a recent article from Fast Company about 533 million accounts getting breached on Facebook https://www.businessinsider.com/stolen-data-of-533-million-facebook-users-leaked-online-2021-4?r=US&IR=T (17).

**Instagram:**  We follow a ton of profiles on Instagram, such as celebrities, sports teams, brands, surfing, hacking, hotrods, motorcycles, news, and family. Facebook owns Instagram. Again, like with FaceBook, think about what you are sharing and to whom.  Here is a great article entitled "Here's Why Hackers Want Your Instagram Account" at https://abc7news.com/abc-7-abc7-seven-on-your-side-michael-finney/5486854/ (18).

**LinkedIn:** LinkedIn is owned by Microsoft. We really enjoy LinkedIn and consider ourselves heavy users of the app. LinkedIn tells people you are connected to about your career, where you have worked, publications, where you volunteer, and the endorsement you have received. Hackers are using LinkedIn to create better phishing attacks. Social engineers or someone with a fake identity will approach you to gain access to where you work. Take a few minutes to read this article about how LinkedIn is used for phishing attacks, https://www.thesslstore.com/blog/hackers-are-using-linkedin-to-tailor-their-phishing-attacks-just-for-you/ (19).

**Twitter:** Twitter is such an interesting concept. You have 240 characters to share your thoughts. Twitter is an amazing resource for learning about people. It's not unusual to prepare for a meeting by looking at someone's Twitter feed and LinkedIn profile to get a baseline of who they are and what they care about.

One of our favorite videos is https://www.youtube.com/watch?v=AyTHVcds6_0 (20). Take a quick look at this video about hacking before moving onto the next section. Now, let's continue our journey on how social engineers collect data on you.

We will now look at the following areas:

- Insider Threats
- Emotional Reaction
- Open Source Intelligence
- Body language

## Insider Threats

We began speaking about this earlier in the book, where Henry shared the experience of physically accessing a large technology company in Silicon Valley.  There are two kinds of insider threats: employees and subcontractors. Review this one-minute video from Cybersecurity & Infrastructure Security Agency (CISA) regarding Insider threats and how these attacks manifest in your organization. https://www.cisa.gov/insider-threat-trailer-and-video (21). This article lays the foundation for insider threats and helps describe 4 defensive strategies. https://www.exabeam.com/ueba/insider-threats/ (22).

## Employees

Too many organizations view cyber as just a thing for the technology department to handle.  Please do not believe this myth.  The number one way hackers get into an organization is through people. Companies need to do a better job of informing their employees.

A company called Right Hand AI uses an adaptive-game-like format on your laptop or mobile device to teach people cyber training in a different way.  There are resources like NINJIO that do a great job of sharing a 3-5 minute animated video describing cyber attacks. Here is a NINJIO video on the cyber security concerns of working from home. https://www.youtube.com/watch?v=nVzPraG-Nzcon (23). Properly trained employees can be one of your organization's front lines of cyber defense. However, if an employee doesn't know what a phishing email looks like or has not been trained properly, they could mistakingly allow a hacker or social engineer into your organization.

If you are an employer, it is also important to remind people who signed NDAs, that, as part of their employment with your company, what is appropriate to share about your company on their social profiles as well as to the public. For example, is it okay for your employees to work on  company documents in a coffee shop using public wifi?

Several years ago I was speaking with a chief information officer after a major powder keg situation erupted in their organization.  There was a cybersecurity hack and a very bad political situation. Yes, I am being vague on purpose.

The CIO told me that despite the public outcry, political upheaval, and breach of data, one of the larger threats to their organization was employees putting out information on their personal Twitter feeds. (Jimmy speaking)

## Subcontractors, Visitors, and Guests

Be mindful of subcontractors and visitors in your organization.  Many times these people can move freely in your facility and are given access to things they should not. A few years ago, we were at a hacker conference. It was late Saturday evening and time to load up our conference gear and set design into our truck. We had our conference badge hung around our necks,  hacker t-shirt on, blue jeans, and athletic shoes. We also had a parking ID badge on display.  Our goal was to get access to an elevator large enough that we could get everything in one trip.

After asking the conference managers for help and no response, we decided to take matters into our own hands. We started looking for any open door in the production area of the conference where we could enter.  We found one door and began walking in the service hallways of this huge building.  We finally found someone on the staff and approached them in a warm, friendly way, just looking for help.  The staff member had a very specific name on his name tag that referenced one of our favorite movies. Looking to connect with this person, we asked him about his name and if he was a motorhead (someone who loves fast cars, hot rods, and motorcycles). In fact, he was a motorhead.  We talked for a good 10 minutes about cars and trucks.  We even got to see a picture of his truck. Eventually we told the staff person our problem and he took us to meet a few more people on his team.  No one ever validated who we were. Did we really have security access to be in this building?  We were able to load up everything in this giant elevator. We were amazed that no one really validated who we were, so we decided to push a bit more :)

Near the security office, there was a free cafeteria for all employees. It was really late, and we were thirsty.  We got in line and helped ourselves to a beverage. It wasn't until we put our cups on the tray to get cleaned, that someone in security finally asked, "who are you?"  They gave us a light scolding for drinking their milk and we went on our merry way.  The point is that we had unrestricted access to a large organization because no one verified who we were.

**Open Source Intelligence (OSINT)** is gathering information and data that is publicly available. There are sources and techniques people can utilize to gain information on a target or mark. There are many books out there on this subject. We highly recommend _Open Source Intelligence Techniques by Michael Bazzell 9th edition._ The book uses top-notch resources for searching for online data. This website discusses in more depth the definition of OSINT. https://www.recordedfuture.com/open-source-intelligence-definition (23a).

Organizations need to be aware of their employees who wear company logos and branded clothing. People, for the most part, are trusting and will believe you if you are wearing company gear with the brand or logo. Not too long ago, there was a story in the news about a non-Verizon employee wearing a Verizon t-shirt at a white supremacist rally. This tarnished the reputation of the company in a big way. We want to share that it's important only to give official company brands to official employees. Social Engineers could use these tactics to gain access and use them against the company. (24)

**Now What? Testing Your Team**

The goal of this chapter was to share with you how social engineering works and the impact it can have on your personal and work life. If you are running a business or government department, you may want to consider how to train your team to be aware of social engineering attacks. Social Engineering Campaigns are set up to trick you and test your abilities to recognize a phishing scam.

**Walk Through**

At the end of the day, you just want to show your team, colleagues, family, and friends how to think differently about social engineering and areas where they are vulnerable. In addition to the items listed above to test your team, you may want to consider having someone test the security of their physical environment.  Send a random stranger through the front door or through the loading docks. Share feedback with your team on how a stranger can access your company from:

- Vibes and sounds, overall environment, displayed feelings and emotions from employees that could be exploited to trigger a reaction.
- Perception of employees' body language.  Were people welcoming to access information, or did they give off language that they are not interested in and will block access to company information?

- Impersonation (pretending you are someone else electronically, via phone, or in person)
- Gossip and Disgruntled Employees often share their loudly and publicly their frustrations.
- Fake emails or spear phishing. Who opened the emails you sent?
- Looking in the trash for information, a.k.a dumpster diving.  (Jimmy speaking)This may sound far-fetched to some, but I kid you not; when writing this section, I had someone go through my trashcans.  Let me tell you the story really quickly.  As I tucked away to bed, one of my family members told me someone was in front of our house going through the trash. Watching through the window, I saw an unknown person with a hard hat on and a light strapped to it (kinda like the Minions wear) going through our trash cans.  By simply yelling out the window for the person to stop going through our trash, they got in their car and drove off.  Super weird.  Always be aware of what you put in the trash.  People are watching and looking for information!

**Is Impersonation Legally and Morally Right?**

Sock puppets are used in creating fictional people. Social engineers use account creation tools to create sock puppets by manipulating data to gain your trust and take full advantage of you and your family. Using generative adversarial networks (GAN), we can learn how to create realistic-looking fake versions of almost anything, as shown by this collection of sites https://thisxdoesnotexist.com/ (25):

- (26) https://thispersondoesnotexist.com/
- (27)  https://www.fakenamegenerator.com/
- (28) https://www.dating-profile-generator.org.uk/
- (29) https://thisrentaldoesnotexist.com/

Suggestion to all, don't steal and don't lie. Literally, if you avoid these two things, your life will be better. However, many people do lie and steal. We want to address the legalities of impersonating people or stealing credentials from dead people.  It mostly depends on what you do with the fake identity and if you break the law. While using a randomly generated name does not constitute identity theft, it may qualify as fraud if you use the fake identity to impersonate someone who's not actually you or otherwise trick people into believing you are someone else.

The term ghosting is used when someone takes the deceased's personal information, in most cases to access money.

The State of California has a special website dedicated to identity theft and the deceased at https://oag.ca.gov/idtheft/facts/deceased (30). The federal government keeps a Death Master File (DMF) of all deceased people. The goal is to stop people from fraudulently accessing deceased people's data. https://dmf.ntis.gov (31).

USA Today and the Detroit Free Press ran a story about a man who stole over $500K, posing as a deceased person. The article also cites other cases of this happening all over the country. https://www.usatoday.com/story/news/nation/2019/10/02/feds-target-social-security-scammers-living-off-dead-relatives/3841975002/ (32).

**Before we head to the next chapter . . .**

Our goal in this chapter is to show how social engineers are experts in manipulating your emotions and taking advantage of the circumstance of the day. We know this was a big chapter to read with a ton of data; however, it is vital that the everyday person understand what is proverbially waiting and lurking behind the next corner of the Internet, text, or social medial site.

When power keg situations erupt, there are those that will profit and take advantage of the situation.  Whether it is a protest, fire, or even an online fundraising campaign to help a deserving person, be on your guard.  You have now been informed.  Always verify. As the former White House Chief of Staff and Mayor of Chicago said, "never let a good crisis go to waste."  During COVID, this was the mantra for many social engineers. The pandemic was used to scam and trick people out of money and spread fear. Later in the book, we will share with you some tools and tactics on how to protect yourself.

**Exercises**

This was, for sure, a heavy chapter, and yes, we are giving homework but it's good homework.  Pick a person you don't know and see what you can learn about them via Facebook, LinkedIn, TikTok, Google Searches, Twitter, Instagram, etc…

We really like Alethe Denis and "Phishy Little Liars." https://www.youtube.com/watch?v=_G19KD5CrEU (33). Make sure to check out her stuff.  She does a great job of explaining how people will create a "pretext" to attack you.

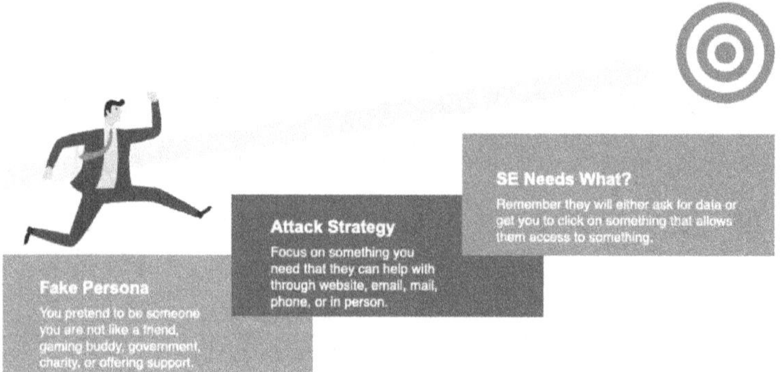


This graphic (above) gives you an idea of how hackers operate.

Many years ago, I (Jimmy) served as a chaplain in a big city jail, working with kids.  I also want to say that working as a chaplain is awesome, and I got to see amazing things happen for kids that got dealt some super-tough cards.

One of the lessons I will never forget is what they told us about Facebook.  Although some of the kids were eager for change, some were not and would use a chaplain to pass information to the outside or to their gang, unknowingly.  As chaplains, we were warned to remove pictures of our family and homes from our Facebook profiles, for our own protection.

**Why?**

The short answer is that personal information can be leveraged. If you want someone to do something, just threaten their family or show up where they live. That's why I started taking down pictures and limiting my online information.  We have already talked about how much you share and show.  I am amazed at how many people I know are in tech and still show personal information online. This can be pictures and videos of their home, events for their kids, their kids' rooms, front and back yards, foods they eat, and when they vacation. This information can be used against you. Be careful what you share with strangers and with what tech companies that give you a FREE service do with your photos and data privacy.

## Website References

We realize there are many ways and styles to cite web references. We think the easiest way is to just copy and select the URL into your browser. This book was written over two years.  Please note that we don't have control if content and links change over time.

(1) https://www.fbi.gov/video-repository/protected-voices-social-engineering-083018.mp4/view

(2) https://www.youtube.com/watch?v=8rrpVtnV_wM

(3) https://corporate.target.com/press/releases/2013/12/target-confirms-unauthorized-access-to-payment-car

(4) https://gatefy.com/blog/real-and-famous-cases-social-engineering-attacks/

(5) https://www.howtogeek.com/465416/what-is-an-internet-troll-and-how-to-handle-trolls/

(6) https://en.wikipedia.org/wiki/Troll_farm

(7) https://www.sciencealert.com/fake-accounts-are-constantly-manipulating-what-you-see-on-social-media-here-s-how

(8) https://www.missingkids.org/ourwork/publications#exploited

(9) https://hbr.org/2016/07/how-to-negotiate-with-a-liar?

cm_sp=Article-_-Links-_-Comment

(10)    https://thispersondoesnotexist.com/

(11)    https://www.wired.com/story/iran-hackers-social-

engineering-mia-ash/

(12)    https://www.youtube.com/watch?v=3U8w58022TA

(12a) https://www.ehacking.net/2021/04/the-ultimate-sock-

puppets-tutorial-for-osint-operators.html

(13)    https://www.apple.com/privacy/docs/

A_Day_in_the_Life_of_Your_Data.pdf

(14)    https://www.youtube.com/watch?

v=YgKz_KLE_yk&t=110s

(15)    https://www.facebook.com/help/212802592074644

(16)    https://help.instagram.com/
contact/505535973176353

(17)    https://www.businessinsider.com/stolen-data-

of-533-million-facebook-users-leaked-online-2021-4?

r=US&IR=T

(18)    https://abc7news.com/abc-7-abc7-seven-on-your-

side-michael-finney/5486854/

(19)    https://www.thesslstore.com/blog/hackers-are-

using-linkedin-to-tailor-their-phishing-attacks-just-for-you/

(20)    https://www.youtube.com/watch?v=AyTHVcds6_0

(21)    https://www.cisa.gov/insider-threat-trailer-and-video

(22)    https://www.exabeam.com/ueba/insider-threats/

(23)    https://www.youtube.com/watch?v=nVzPraG-Nzc

(23a) https://www.recordedfuture.com/open-source-intelligence-definition

(24) https://www.huffpost.com/entry/verizon-charlottesville_n_599605dfe4b0e8cc855c69ee

(25) https://thisxdoesnotexist.com/

(26) https://thispersondoesnotexist.com/

(27) https://www.fakenamegenerator.com/

(28) https://www.dating-profile-generator.org.uk/

29) https://thisrentaldoesnotexist.com/

(30) https://oag.ca.gov/idtheft/facts/deceased

(31) https://dmf.ntis.gov

(32) https://www.usatoday.com/story/news/nation/2019/10/02/feds-target-social-security-scammers-living-off-dead-relatives/3841975002/

(33) https://www.youtube.com/watch?v=_G19KD5CrEU

(34) https://usa.kaspersky.com/resource-center/definitions/pharming

(35) https://www.phishlabs.com/blog/brain-hacking-social-engineering-effective/

(36) https://www.behindthename.com

(37) https://www.fakenamegenerator.com/gen-random-us-us.php

(38) https://www.elfqrin.com/fakeid.php

(39) https://www.bleepingcomputer.com/news/security/mfa-fatigue-hackers-new-favorite-tactic-in-high-profile-breaches/

# Chapter 4

# HOW TO KNOW IF YOU ARE GETTING SOCIALLY ENGINEERED

We are three chapters into the book, and there is more coming. The topic is relevant, and by now, you are becoming aware of how people may be socially engineered. This next chapter is going to focus on the following areas:

✓ Becoming Fraud Aware

✓ Knowing Where to Go to Look for Help

✓ Quick Bootcamp on Verifying Links, Emails, Texts, Phone Numbers, and Deepfakes

There is an old saying that if it walks like a duck, or swims like a duck, that it is probably a duck.  However, in social engineering, you can not rely on this old adage.

**Becoming Fraud Aware**

One of the may ingredients of a social engineer or any con is to offer something someone wants or needs while executing a deception plan to complete a nefarious goal or mission. We have learned that fear, greed, lack of resources, panic, illness, and loneliness are ways to access people or their systems.  Many penetration testers (someone whose job it is to try to get someone to click on a link) and hackers have shared with me that when they go after an organization, they may send thousands of emails and texts, but they only need one person to accidentally click, and they are in your network. Let's go back to our old buddy, James Kumah, from earlier in the book and his polite request to ask us for help. Take a few minutes and look at this letter and revisit why this looks sketchy. We put in bold some words that we should be concerned about.

"Dear Friend.

My name is Mr James Kumah. I write to seek your services in a **private and confidential matter regarding an unaccounted fund in our bank here in Ghana** during the last two years 2018 end of the year's report. As a Regional Manager in this Bank, I deposited this fund in an **ESCROW CALL ACCOUNT at our headquarters pending when I shall get a reliable person. This requires a private arrangement.   Could you perhaps be able to receive these funds under legal claims then I will file you in.** I will appreciate for fewer questions asked and your participation will be 40%  of the total money. **There are practically no risks involved,** the transaction will be **executed under a legitimate arrangement** that will protect you from any breach of the law, it will be simply a bank-to-bank transfer. I have all the details and will file you in if you are really willing. **Your major role would be to provide an existing account or open a new bank account where the funds** will be transferred and stand as the original depositor of this fund in our bank, as long as you will **remain honest to me till the end for this important business trusting in you and believing that you will never let me down either now or in future.** Once this fund is transferred into your account, I shall resign from my job and bring my family to start a new life in your country.**The funds in question are quite**

**large, Twelve million five hundred thousand United States Dollars. ($12,500,000.00).** I will expect a straight answer from you. If yes, please get back to me so that we can work out the modalities without further delay.

I will be monitoring the whole situation here in this bank until you confirm the money in your account and ask me to come down to your country for subsequent sharing of the fund according to percentages previously indicated and further investment, either in your country or any country you advice us to invest in. All other necessary vital information will be sent to you when I hear from you I look forward to receive your email. Regards. Mr James Kumah"

The letter above is pretty obviously a scam. However, he may have convinced one person to pull the trigger. During the time we were writing this chapter, we recieved a text from the DMV stating, "Hi it's Jamie from the Motorvehicle Dept. We just issued a ruling that qualifies you to collect a Refund_Payment: Average refund $800." Jamie was also kind enough to share a link we  could click on if we wanted the $800.  Go back over the text, and look for typos and states of phrases.  We literally copied the message verbatim.  By the way, there is no $800; it is a scam to get access to your phone and information.

People fall on hard times. We personally know people who are struggling. $800 may be the difference someone needs to pay their rent, stop a car from being repossessed, keep the lights on, or put much-needed groceries on the table. There are numerous reports stating that people have been getting depressed from spending too much time on social media, being isolated, and having difficulty filtering what is true from all of the negative social media and political propaganda.  So it is not too far-fetched for someone who is not in a good mental place, has massive stress, and is worried to click on the link.

**Watch Dogs - Where to Go to Keep Up to Speed on the Latest Scams**

Let's examine a five-year period of scams.

**2017-2022**

The Federal Trade Commission (FTC) is focused on protecting the American consumer. According to the FTC 2017 Consumer Sentinel Network Data Book, the top ten fraud categories are listed on the next page.

| RANK | CATEGORY | # OF REPORTS | % REPORTING $ LOSS | TOTAL AMOUNT LOSS | MEDIAN $ LOSS |
| --- | --- | --- | --- | --- | --- |
| 1 | Imposter Scams | 347,829 | 19% | $328M | $500 |
| 2 | Telephone and Mobile Services | 149,578 | 4% | $17M | $223 |
| 3 | Prizes, Sweepstakes and Lotteries | 142,870 | 9% | $95M | $511 |
| 4 | Shop-at-Home and Catalog Sales | 126,387 | 58% | $94M | $261 |
| 5 | Internet Services | 45,093 | 14% | $19M | $183 |
| 6 | Foreign Money Offers & Counterfeit Check Scams | 31,980 | 33% | $34M | $1,008 |
| 7 | Travel, Vacations, and Timeshare Plans | 22,264 | 18% | $38M | $1,710 |
| 8 | Business and Job Opportunities | 18,702 | 34% | $47M | $1,063 |
| 9 | Advance Payments for Credit Services | 17,762 | 74% | $15M | $318 |
| 10 | Health Care | 10,321 | 8% | $1M | $175 |

Source:<u>https://www.ftc.gov/system/files/documents/reports/</u> <u>consumer-sentinel-network-data-book-2017/</u> <u>consumer_sentinel_data_book_2017.pdf</u> (1).

The list on the previous page is pretty impressive.  We are being told to pay attention to their top-ten areas of scams. We have covered most all of these in the first few chapters of this book. So the next time you get a text, email, or call about any of the following areas, beware:

1.  Imposter Scams
2.  Mobile Services
3.  Games and Sweepstakes
4.  Home Shopping
5.  Internet Services
6.  Foreign Money Offer
7.  Travel and Timeshares
8.  Job and Business Opportunities
9.  Advance Payments
10. Healthcare

In 2019 the FTC highlighted Network data having 1.7 million fraud reports, and the top three categories are

1. Identity Theft
2. Imposter Scams
3. Telephone & Mobile Services.

Source: ftc.gov https://www.ftc.gov/reports/consumer-sentinel-network-data-book-2019

In 2020, this report showed fraud losses at $3.3B. Let's move ahead to 2021. Look at the numbers below. I am sure you can see that the numbers keep getting bigger.

Source: ftc.gov https://www.ftc.gov/reports/consumer-sentinel-network-data-book-2021

Across the U.S., there are constant warnings from federal and state governments about ongoing scams. Below are highlights of some of the many scams going on throughout America.


- In August of 2021, the US Department of Health and Human Services' inspector general lets the public know to be aware of fraud schemes related to COVID. "Scammers are using telemarketing calls, text messages, social media platforms, and door-to-door visits to perpetrate COVID-19-related scams." https://oig.hhs.gov/fraud/consumer-alerts/fraud-alert-covid-19-scams/ (2).
- In May of 2021, State of California Attorney General Bonta issues a consumer alert warning regarding counterfeit COVID-19 Vaccination Record Cards https://oag.ca.gov/news/press-releases/attorney-general-bonta-issues-consumer-alert-warning-californians-about-0 (3).
- In January of 2021, The State of Texas Comptroller has a fraud alert section on the website. Businesses participating in the Central Master Bidders List (CMBL) reported a phishing scam claiming to be from the comptroller's office that was not associated with their agency. The CMBL consists of manufacturers, suppliers, and other vendors doing business with the state, who bid

on government contracts. https://comptroller.texas.gov/fraud-alert/  (4)

- In August of 2020, then State of California Attorney General Xavier Becerra issued a warning of digital scams stating, "Recently, unscrupulous actors have impersonated well-known politicians, celebrities, and business executives on social media and YouTube channels in "giveaway" scams that falsely promised, for example, to double any digital assets sent to a specific digital asset wallet. These schemes are only the most recent example of attempts by scam artists to capitalize on novel technologies in order to rob Californians of their hard-earned savings. https://oag.ca.gov/news/press-releases/attorney-general-becerra-warns-investors-and-consumers-beware-digital-asset  (5).

- In April 2020, the Federal Trade Commission Blog on stimulus payment scams stated, "Scammers are using these stimulus payments to try to rip people off. They might try to get you to pay a fee to get your stimulus payment. Or they might try to convince you to give them your Social Security number, bank account, or government benefits debit card account number. " https://www.consumer.ftc.gov/blog/2020/04/coronavirus-stimulus-payment-scams-what-you-need-know  (6).

- In March 2020, the FBI issues a public service
  announcement regarding the rise in fraudulent COVID-19
  scams stating, "Scammers are leveraging the COVID-19
  pandemic to steal your money, your personal information,
  or both. Don't let them. Protect yourself and do your
  research before clicking on links purporting to provide
  information on the virus; donating to a charity online or
  through social media; contributing to a crowdfunding
  campaign; purchasing products online; or giving up your
  personal information in order to receive money or other
  benefits."   https://www.ic3.gov/media/2020/200320.aspx
  (7).
- State of Michigan AG Consumer Alerts has a dedicated
  web page for Government Imposter Scams providing
  information on fake government emails and texts, IRS
  scams, winning lottery notices, debt collection, and fake
  government grants. https://www.michigan.gov/ag/
  0,4534,7-359-81903_20942-390419--,00.html (8).
- The "Phish Tank" at Berkeley is another great resource to
  keep up on the latest phishing scams. https://
  security.berkeley.edu/resources/phish-tank  (9).

**Even when watchdogs and the world is watching . . .**

Another type of environment hackers will use are natural disasters. In a recent interview on the California Cybersecurity Institute's YouTube page, Ron Snyder from Cisco is interviewed. Ron is a solutions architect for Cisco's crisis response team. When a disaster strikes, Ron's team will help provide communications support. The interview delves into some of the areas they have provided support to throughout the country in areas such as Ecuador and the Philippines. The interview points out that when natural disaster strikes, we will see the best and the worst of humanity.  Many times cybercriminals will exploit disaster situations to access information.

**How to Know if I am Getting Scammed**

Research has shown it's difficult to sense when you are being socially engineered, scammed, or conned. Many times online communication lacks the normal cues we would pick up by looking at someone using the Albert Mehrabian 7-35-55 communication model and principle mentioned earlier in the book. Think about it as if one had the ability to really see who or what was sending the message.

Apple has a dedicated website for Expanded Protections for Children at https://www.apple.com/child-safety/ (10). We will talk more about this later in the book when we discuss Social Martial Arts.  Take some time to read this web page.  Apple states on this page that they want to help protect kids from predators and limit the spread of Child Sexual Abuse Material (CASM).  Again, we will talk more about this later, but Apple is using technology to help give parents and kids insight into dangerous content.

The idea here is that when we can't see someone face to face, we can't pick up on cues that would tell us to run or make us concerned.  Many social engineers will use advanced psychological tactics to make someone do an action or gain access to information.

Earlier in the book, we cited a study from Malcom Gladwell's book "Talking to Strangers" about how it can be hard to detect if someone is telling the truth or not. Many times people will get attacked when they are in a fragile state or extremely angry. We all have had something put over on us at one time or another.

If you have been scammed or are currently involved in a possible scam, don't be ashamed. Repeat that.  Don't be ashamed. Just get help even if you are being threatened.

Most federal, state, and local policing organizations have a cybercrime division.  Many organizations, like banks, have resources to help. The point is to get help.  Whether you are an employer, parent, or employee, make sure those you care about are informed and trained. Stick with us to the end of the book, where we have "Social Martial Arts " resources. For now, we want to look at links, emails, texts, phone messages, and deepfakes.

## Links

By now, you are starting to get the idea that someone may try to run a scam and send you a link that can do some damage. Here are a few guidelines to check if a link is there to scam you or is legit.

✓ Don't open the link.
✓ Look for spelling or grammar mistakes that seem off or not quite right.
✓ Take your cursor and hold it over the link. Do not click on it. Is it a different link than what it claims to be?  This is a good indicator that something phishy is happening.
✓ You can use several online services to reverse look of any phone number associated with the email or text to confirm validity. Most of these sites have a fee; however,

a few dollars spent in the short term could save you in the long term.

✓ If a link does not use traditional naming conventions. Sometimes shorter emails that don't follow traditional website naming conventions are a sign that something is wrong. As I am writing this section of the book, I got a text message saying, "Your USPS delivery with tracked code 48711 is waiting to set delivery preferences", and the link 5odk.info/HwZDTO5JqB was included for me to click on.  Now the link looks sketchy, but I wanted to double-check my hunch, so I went over to  https://unmask.sucuri.net/security-report/  (11)  and typed in the address "5odk.info/HwZDTO5JqB".  You guessed it, there was a suspicious script found in the link.

**Texts**

When you get a new phone number, don't be surprised if you get smished like crazy. **Smishing** is a form of Phishing, but through text messaging instead of email. Often the text message is from a seemingly reliable source offering money or a refund. In chapter three, you may recall we shared the following examples of questionable texts.

- *"This is Ava Mae from Quick Lend and I have been permitted to offer you a potential pre approval for up to $1800.  Please complete your docs"*
- *"This is from USPS (United States Postal Office) concerning a a schedule deliver. Read here (website link) Robert."* Not a great idea to send to Jimmy or Henry :) !!!
- *"This Jane S from customer service and I have been authorized to offer you a potential pre approval for up to $2380. Please view your forms."* BTW much better deal than Ava Mae :).
- *"This is yours, We found a refund payment of $681.25 is due to you on your insurance Policy. Claim REFUND HERE:"*
- *"DMV NOTICE: You only have 48 hours left to receive your $927 Refund payment from the Motor Vehicle Dpt. Please do it immediately"*
- *"Due to the pandemic, Hulu is giving everyone a free 1-year subscription to help you stay at home. Get yours here"*
- *"This I Jo Ellen from customer service, and I have been authorized to offer you a potential pre-approval for up to $3250.  Please view your forms"*

- ***"Dear Loyal AT&T customer, please take a couple of minutes and claim your $100 at the end of this survey."***

As we discussed earlier, we are purposely leaving out the URLs. With all American carriers, you can forward suspicious text messages to 7726 to report it.

Another thing to look for with smishing are the numbers that appear in the text message. The number will look like a personal cellphone number instead of the commonly used 5-digit marketing number, like 5000. If you don't know the person or recognize the number, don't engage.

When we get a questionable text message, here is what we do instantly. We block the contact and any numbers associated with the text. Always delete emails you are unfamiliar with.  If there are suspicious links and actions to click on a website, please stay clear and do not click.

If you do click on the link, reboot your phone, and delete all web history. It may not hurt to install a VPN on your phone like Tunnel Bear or Nord VPN.  Turn off Bluetooth and delete any financial information on your phone stored for payment.

You may want to let your financial institution and credit card providers know as well.

**Phone**

Remember the screaming baby video mentioned at the beginning of the book where a social engineer called the cell phone provider, stating that she was buying her first house and her husband had not added her to the account?  She quickly got added to the account where she could change the password.  Keep in mind that your email address and phone number are out there through a variety of social sites. That information can be used by social engineers.

When using your phone we recommend not answering calls from unknown numbers or ones that are flagged as spam.

Besides phone calls, the modern cell phone is also a computer. Many people store their credit cards, health care information, access to work portals, contacts, and photos. We suggest taking the time to go through the security settings of your phone.  For example, don't let any app have access to your camera, microphone, or contacts. It is very possible for someone to access your camera, listen to you through the phone mic, and get information from your phone.

Remember, someone can steal your accounts and then sell them for profit.

Be aware of the apps you download on your phone. When was the last time you downloaded an app and paid attention to whether it was secure or not?  I (Jimmy) was on the phone with a healthcare provider, who encouraged me to download their app for better, quicker, and faster service.  I asked if their app was secure and got the standard "company" answer that didn't reassure me. I pushed back and asked how do you know that if I give your company and app access to my phone that we can be sure the medical information is secure? I didn't get an answer from customer service, but I did look up the company and recent breaches. All I can say is "not good."

There are currently over three million apps you can download.  Back in 2016, you may remember the Uber breach involving the data of 57 million people using the app and another 600,000 drivers for the company. And yes, we definitely had Uber on our phones back then.  As business travelers, Uber is a must-have app. Take a few minutes to read this article on NPR about the breach and legal claim that impacted Uber at https://www.npr.org/

<u>2018/09/27/652119109/uber-pays-148-million-over-year-
long-cover-up-of-data-breach</u> (12).

Our point is to encourage you to do some homework about an app before you download it.  Just because an app is available to download from a company's site does not mean it is safe or secure. We love the convenience of phone apps but remember that you may be giving your information to an organization that does not have strong security controls in place. Take a look at how many downloads the app has.  An app with millions of downloads means many people have used it.  See if there are frequently asked questions and read the app privacy policy.  Good companies explain what they do with your data. In the event your phone gets stolen, you may want to remotely wipe the data from your phone. Do a quick search on this in any browser, and you will get lots of options.

One more thing on phones . . .

We suggest doing the following when you go out in public:
1.  Turn your Bluetooth off while not in use.
2.  Set up your lock screen, password/or biometric features to lock/unlock your phone.
3.  Turn off location services (GPS) & SIRI or ALEXA.

4.  Don't accept pairing requests from devices you don't know. Set Airdrop to "Allow me to be discovered by no one."

5.  Don't use public wifi.

6.  Look at all your phone's security features and use things like two-factor authentication.

7.  Set Up Remote Device Location and Remote Wipe.

8.  Turn the phone off daily. (to reset Cell towers)

9.  Be mindful of your surroundings. I always take a quick look around and make sure there are no obvious signs of someone having a portable hacking kit in a backpack.

10. Remove apps that you do not use.

11. Keep Software Up to Date.

12. Secure your Browser.  https://us-cert.cisa.gov/publications/securing-your-web-browser  (13).


Remember, when you are jumping in your car or truck to go somewhere, get in the habit of turning off your Bluetooth to prevent unwanted people from connecting to you and your car. How many of us connect our phones to our cars without asking if the car's network is safe, secure, and reliable?


You may think this sounds extreme, but is merely being aware of your surroundings/situational awareness. Remember, your Bluetooth settings can be discovered by anyone that is in your range. Let's run through some Bluetooth definitions.

**Bluebugging** is where a hacker will access your phone's information via the process when two devices connect together.

**Bluejacking** is when you get messages from a source you do not know. The key here is they are just sending messages.

**Bluesnarfing** is when someone gets on your phone and takes information.

**Deepfakes**

Research has shown it's difficult to sense when you are being socially engineered, scammed, or conned. Listen to this fascinating podcast (15:26) with Maria Konnikova as she discusses the psychology of con artists and hackers. She says you can never be prepared, and you never see them coming https://thecyberwire.com/ podcasts/hacking-humans/73/notes (16).

"The reason it's called a deepfake is that it's not exactly the same and actually side-by-side, they sound similar, but not identical, but independently, without the reference of the original, it starts to sound almost identical, right? 2021 Deep Fake with Tom Cruise https://www.abc.net.au/news/2021-06-24/tom-cruise-deepfake-chris-ume-security-washington-dc/100234772 (14). *There's no anchor to be like, "That's not real," which I think is part of what's dangerous about the deep fake technology is that without the original, we don't really know... We're like, "Gosh, that sounds like..." And our mind defaults to truth.  So our brain defaults to the fact like, "Oh, it sounds close enough." And our brain's like, "Yeah, that's close enough." (14).*

Review this course: Linked In Learning Course Understanding the Impact of Deepfake Videos to learn more about deepfakes. https://www.linkedin.com/learning/understanding-the-impact-of-deepfake-videos  (15).

Con artists use deepfakes on dating websites to prey on your vulnerabilities. Let's review this FBI website to break down Romance Scams and how they prey on people. https://www.fbi.gov/scams-and-safety/common-scams-and-crimes/romance-scams (17).

We have to be aware that people can create videos that sound similar to the actual person. Have you ever watched a spy movie where a person creates a video of a person and, using technology, has the person say things that are not theirs?  Think of it this way; a deepfake uses everything we talked about earlier in the book with the 7-38-55 principle to make it look like it is real.

People post videos and images of themselves all the time. With modern technology, it is possible to clone someone's voice and image. You may have heard the term AI which stands for artificial intelligence. AI is everywhere. People are using AI to go through the massive tons of data that are in the digital world and look for certain things (sensors). Before diving into the details on deepfake videos, spend some time with this blog entitled "14 Deepfake Examples that Terrified and Amused the Internet." https://www.creativebloq.com/features/deepfake-examples  (18).

According to a blog on Facebook's website, "Facebook, the Partnership on AI, Microsoft, and academics from Technical University of Munich, University of Naples Federico II, Cornell Tech, MIT, University of Oxford, UC Berkeley, University of Maryland, College Park, and University at

Albany–SUNY" launched the Deepfake Detection Challenge in September of 2019 (source https://ai.facebook.com/blog/deepfake-detection-challenge-results-an-open-initiative-to-advance-ai/). The competition's goal was "to accelerate the development of new ways to detect deepfake videos." The competition had over 2,000 participants with the opportunity to win prizes totaling one million dollars.

The tech behind deepfakes uses machine learning (ML). An AI learns how to review the pictures and images of a person they plan to target and gathers every detail about them. The human face has over 43 muscles, and it takes around 10 muscles just to smile. If you have AI looking quickly through volumes and volumes of images, it is not too far-fetched to imagine that AI could capture and analyze many of one's facial expressions accurately.

Think about a famous politician or actor. By the nature of their job, they have pictures everywhere. Once the person's face is analyzed, we move to the voice. I want you to think about a famous person out there and people that impersonate them. These people will focus on a few aspects of their personal personality and over-accentuate them for comedic purposes. During the last presidential election,

Saturday Night Live, had a skit where actors impersonated people running for office using deep fakes.

Do you remember the popular app that would show what you look like when you are older? Now being older, we had no desire to see ourselves as really, really old. However, we know lots of young people that got a kick of seeing how they would look older. It seemed innocent, but ultimately the FBI found that this particular app originated in Russia and was a security risk.

There are a number of tools (some free) that can create deepfake videos. If you recall the 7-38-55 principle, the visual is super important, but so is the sound of a person. After AI is taught the tone and pitch of a person's speech, it can eventually emulate how a person speaks.

We encourage you to watch https://moondisaster.org (19). "In Event of Moon Disaster is an immersive art project inviting you into alternative history, asking us all to consider how new technologies can bend, redirect and obfuscate the truth around us. To construct the story, a variety of techniques of misinformation were used – from simple deceptive editing to more complex deepfake technologies. To recreate the contingency speech, the piece used deep learning techniques to create both a synthetic voice of Nixon and to use dialogue replacement techniques to replicate the movement of Nixon's mouth and lips. By creating this alternative history, the project explores the influence and pervasiveness of misinformation and deep fake technologies in our contemporary society."

We want you to be aware of deepfakes the next time there is a "powder keg" situation going on in the world. Think about how AI now has the ability to create fraudulent videos quickly and spread misinformation. If you have a concern about a video or picture, make sure to do some homework before reacting.

There are a number of sites you can use to help gain more insight on deepfake.  You can visit https://www.factcheck.org (20) or https://www.youtube.com/channel/ UCGf4OIX_aTt8DlrgiH3jN3g (21).

## Website References

We realize there are many ways and styles to cite web references. We think the easiest way is to just copy and select the URL into your browser. This book was written over two years.  Please note that we don't have the control if content and links change over time.

(1) https://www.ftc.gov/system/files/documents/reports/consumer-sentinel-network-data-book-2017/consumer_sentinel_data_book_2017.pdf

(2) https://oig.hhs.gov/fraud/consumer-alerts/fraud-alert-covid-19-scams/

(3) https://oag.ca.gov/news/press-releases/attorney-general-bonta-issues-consumer-alert-warning-californians-about-0

(4) https://comptroller.texas.gov/fraud-alert/

(5) https://oag.ca.gov/news/press-releases/attorney-general-becerra-warns-investors-and-consumers-beware-digital-asset

(6) https://www.consumer.ftc.gov/blog/2020/04/coronavirus-stimulus-payment-scams-what-you-need-know

(7) https://www.ic3.gov/media/2020/200320.aspx

(8) https://www.michigan.gov/ag/
0,4534,7-359-81903_20942-390419--,00.html

(9) https://security.berkeley.edu/resources/phish-tank

(10) https://www.apple.com/child-safety/

(11) https://unmask.sucuri.net/security-report/

(12) ) https://www.npr.org/2018/09/27/652119109/uber-
pays-148-million-over-year-long-cover-up-of-data-breach

(13)_ https://us-cert.cisa.gov/publications/securing-your-
web-browser

(14) https://www.abc.net.au/news/2021-06-24/tom-cruise-
deepfake-chris-ume-security-washington-dc/100234772

(15) https://www.linkedin.com/learning/understanding-
the-impact-of-deepfake-videos

(16) https://thecyberwire.com/podcasts/hacking-
humans/73/notes

(17) https://www.fbi.gov/scams-and-safety/common-
scams-and-crimes/romance-scams

(18) https://www.creativebloq.com/features/deepfake-
examples

(19) https://moondisaster.org

(20) https://www.factcheck.org

(21) https://www.youtube.com/channel/
UCGf4OIX_aTt8DlrgiH3jN3g

# NOTES

# Chapter 5

# CLICKING AND YOUR DIGITAL DUST

Everyone should know about the CIA Triad and how it relates to your digital dust. Information security or cybersecurity rely on three main security design principles of the CIA triad, also sometimes known as the tenets of cybersecurity.

CIA Triad Information that is secure satisfies three main tenets, or properties, of information. If you can ensure these three tenets, you satisfy the requirements of secure information (Kim & Solomon, 2013).

- Confidentiality- Only authorized users can view information.
- Integrity- Only authorized users can change information.
- Availability- Information is accessible by authorized users whenever they request the information.

Southern New Hampshire University describes these concepts here: https://learn.snhu.edu/d2l/lor/viewer/viewFile.d2lfile/760194/22533,-1/ (31)

**Clicking and Digital Dust**

While we can't protect everyone, all the time, from every kind of attack, we can show you how to lock down your information to protect the perimeter of your tech and the digital footprints that you can leave behind when visiting a website. This chapter will cover the following areas:

- Emitting Digital Dust
- Privacy Agreements
- Protecting Your Data
- What do you share publicly
- Phones and apps
- Stopping unwanted visitors from accessing your devices
- Social Engineering First Aid Kit

We encourage you to not only read this chapter but implement what we are saying. This, by far, is one of the most important chapters of the book. If someone gains access to your personal identification information (PII), they can literally become you.

**Digital Dust and the Physical Impact on Your Body /
Radio Frequency (RF) Exposure Awareness!**

We wanted to alert you that your connection to devices can
be harmful to your physical being.  Exposure to cell phone
radiation is a health risk. The specific absorption rate (SAR)
is how the human body soaks in radio frequency waves. Our
recommendation is to limit your cell phone exposure and
read more about RF exposure.

Are you aware that phone manufacturers must make
available legal and regulatory information regarding RF
exposure and other interesting information? On the Apple
iPhone, to view Legal & Regulatory information (including
legal notices and license, warranty, and RF exposure
information) and regulatory marks, go to Settings >
General > Legal & Regulatory. SAR Ratings and RF
exposure are items we should be aware of. The Federal
Communications Commission (FCC) discusses Specific
Absorption Rate (SAR) For Cell Phones: What it means For
You at https://www.fcc.gov/consumers/guides  and https://
emfacademy.com/check-sar-value-mobile-phone/  (1). SAR
provides a measurement of the RF(radio frequency)
exposure characteristics of cell phones to make sure they

are within the safety guidelines set by the FCC. "All cell phones must meet the FCC's RF exposure standard, which is set well below that at which laboratory testing indicates, and medical and biological experts generally agree, adverse health effects could occur." SAR ratings are mandated to list the SAR rating for their phones. Every cell phone manufacturer is mandated to not only obtain a SAR rating for their phones and report that information to the FCC, but they also must publish that information on their website in a user-friendly way. To figure out the model of your phone (if you don't already know it) look at the back of your phone, in the user manual, or in the general settings of your phone. The EMF website discusses how to find SAR information.

You can also use the manufacturer's website to find out the reported SAR values. Here are links to the SAR value listings of some of the major phone manufacturers to save you some time.

- Apple https://www.apple.com/legal/rfexposure/ (2)

- LG  https://www.lg.com/global/support/sar/sar (3)

- Motorola  https://rfhealth-sar.motorola.com/SAR/ (4)

- Samsung  https://www.samsung.com/sar/sarMain.do (5)

If your phone is made by another company, use your browser to search "(Your Phone Model) SAR Rating" and scroll through the first few search results until you see the actual manufacturer's website.

## How Much Dust Are We Talking About?

A recent blog entitled "8 Social Media Marketing Trends & Predictions for 2022 & Beyond" states that the average person spends 145 minutes a day on social media and has an attention span of about eight seconds. https://blog.red-website-design.co.uk/2022/09/07/social-trends-finish-with-bang/ (6) Think about this alarming stat for a moment. Statista says there are 4.66 billion people actively using the internet. Of the 4.66 billion, 92.6 percent are accessing the internet via their phones.

## Emitting Digital Dust

Protecting yourself and your digital dust or data must be a priority. What you share publicly can seriously harm your digital footprint and profile. Let's break down what we mean by digital dust. We really like this definition by Ema Linaker. https://www.linkedin.com/pulse/what-digital-dust-should-we-worry-ours-ema-linaker/ (7) "Dust, by its very existence, is literally the most material of things. It's what is left of an object when all form, structure, context, and legibility are stripped away — when the object is destroyed, and only the fact of its materiality remains. Therefore, dust would seem to be the antithesis of digital, the opposite of its binary 0s and 1s. Digital means data, virtual and immaterial; it's black and white, crisply demarcated, and perfectly defined. Dust is grey and deeply, existentially fuzzy."

So think of it this way, when you go to a website or interact with an app, chances are you are sharing and/or getting tracked. This is your digital dust. To see the impact of your digital dust please read Gartner's latest report on "2021 Top Strategic Technology Trends; the huge rise in connected devices is leaving a digital 'trace' or 'dust' behind users in terms of preferences, emotions, and behaviors." https://www.gartner.com/en/newsroom/press-releases/2020-10-19-gartner-identifies-the-top-strategic-technology-trends-for-2021 (8).

When you visit a website or download an app, you share digital information with the website. Despite your security settings, you may be sharing your internet protocol address (phone number equivalent to the internet connection of your system), your browser (depending on settings, can reveal a great deal of information about you and your system), with the autofill option, and your browsing history. A recent article by Semrush Blog entitled "Not Just Another Digital Marketing Trends 2022 Post" stated in a section on privacy-driven marketing that "They report that around 80% of users opt-out of tracking from mobile apps they download from the App Store." There is an awakening going on in digital privacy; maybe the 80% reference above is on to something. Data is always being collected. Take a look at webkay.robinlinus.com (9) to see what your browser tells about you.

## How Does Your Digital Dust Get Collected?

As we participate in the digital world and our electronic communities, one must be aware of the risks. A cookie is something delicious that you can eat. In the tech world, a cookie is a file that stores information about you, such as a password. Do you have a frequent site you go to regularly, and it automatically updates your password? Most of us do. Then there are cookies with your information out on the Internet.

Here is another way to think about a cookie in terms of a website.  Have you used valet parking? When you pull up to the valet, you give them your keys to your car, and they give you a ticket.  When you are ready to leave, you walk up to the valet stand and give them the ticket.  Typically part of the ticket is stored on the windshield of your car with some identification on it and the other part of the ticket is given to you, so the valet attendant knows that the car belongs to you.  Think about your favorite online shopping store. You log in, they remember you, and may even share insights into other products you might like to buy.  Cookies are just another way to track you.

When there are ads on a webpage, these are called 3rd party cookies. These ads will have cookies in them that track you also. Here are some areas the cookie monsters look at:

- Marketing cookies to help deliver more ads you might like.
- Performance cookies to understand how you interact with a website
- Functional cookies to better understand how you interact with their website
- Essential cookies (which are good) to make sure you are secure

**How do you defend yourself from the cookie monster?**

Several browsers now automatically block 3rd party cookies. As we see the change in 3rd party cookies, don't forget about 1st party cookies. 1st party cookies store information like your passcodes and preferences for the website. They are sticking around.

We mentioned the 1st and 3rd party cookies. What about 2nd party cookies and data? When cookies collected by one company are shared with another company via some kind of partnership, we call this a 2nd party cookie. Have you ever bought something online, and because of that purchase, you started getting a bunch of targeted advertising?  That's likely because of 2nd party cookies.

We know there has been recent legislation on data privacy; however, we don't see this going away. It has been said that data is the new oil. So there are many companies and individuals out there trying to mine your data.

## Phones and Digital Dust

There is a great deal of research showing that a majority of people access websites from their phones. The modern phone is a powerful computer that you can put in your pocket and access information anytime, anywhere.

The average person spends over 2 hours a day on their phones, how many are locking down their data, understanding privacy policies, and protecting their proverbial digital dust?

Typically on mobile devices, you will have an advertising ID that collects:

1. Your name and email
2. Where you live
3. The device you use
4. Any information you freely gave to them when agreeing to use their stuff
5. They may also add language that they combine current 3rd party data collected with the AdID. Many AdID policies say that they share information with data brokers. Be very aware of the language in your advertising ID, where they may not consider it to be targeted

advertising when they collect info on you for targeted advertising or measurement.  This kinda sounds to me like it is targeted advertising.  You can't have things both ways.  You are either collecting our stuff and using it for targetedadvertising, or you or not.  One of the best pieces of advice is to follow the money trail.

Mobile Devices and cookies technologies are regularly changing how we use cookies on mobile phones. It's recommended that you clear your cookies weekly. Read here about cookies. https://www.allaboutcookies.org/mobile/index.html (10).

Earlier in the book, we gave some examples of what Meta (formerly Facebook) collects on you.  Take a look at what apps want to access on your phone. Are you giving them access to your pictures, mic, and videos? Review through the privacy section of your device.

**Apps and Digital Dust**

We recently attended a webinar entitled "Data Transparency: What Every User Should Know About

Facebook" https://youtu.be/YgKz_KLE_yk (12). This webinar provided a detailed overview of how to protect your information on Facebook. There are multiple resources and news organizations that reference a recent data breach of over 500 million Facebook users. Think about all the personal information that you share on Facebook, and now there is a breach of over 500 million people.  To visualize this, consider the population of the United States of America is approximately 331 million people.  Still not quite 500 million, so let's look for another country or two to help us get to 500 million.  Mexico's population is approximately 129 million.  We are getting closer but still need another 40 million to hit the 500 million mark.  Let's add in Canada, which is 37 million.  So the populations of the US, Mexico, and Canada combined about 497 million people. The recent 500 million person breach would be like if everyone in the countries of USA, Mexico, and Canada were breached.  It's big.

During the webinar, one of the presenters gave an example using Door Dash.  He never used Door Dash through Facebook to order food, yet Facebook had a file on his activity with Door Dash. The presenter, who was in college, went on to say that people his age have a "numbness" when dealing with digital privacy, big data, and targeting.

**Your Friendly Neighborhood Data Privacy Statements - Beware!**

A privacy policy says, "Hey, I am going to collect this data about you and use it for these purposes." You agree to this by clicking "here." Keep in mind that just because a company states, "we don't sell your data," it does not mean that they don't use it to help advertisers target your demographics. We want to be really careful in this section about what we say but pay close attention to how companies are defining what the word "sell" means.

The Pew Research Center at www.pewresearch.org did a study in 2019 on "Americans' attitudes and experiences with privacy policies and laws." This article found that people are asked to look at privacy policies 25 times daily.  If we are looking at the average person spending 145 minutes daily online and we divide 145 by 25, we arrive at 5.8.  So in a person's daily online experience, they are getting hit up every 5 minutes.

It gets worse. Of the people reading privacy policies, Pew research stated that of the ⅔ of the people that read privacy policies, only 55% have "some" understanding.

When you are on social media or interacting with an app, you have to take it seriously and spend time understanding the language in their privacy policy. As another example, in 2023, TikTok bans have been spreading across our country because TikTok has been identified as a national security threat. We took the liberty of reading several websites' privacy policies. Below is a general summary of these privacy statements.

- ☑ Most will give you an explanation of what this organization will do with your data and how it's collected and processed.  Make sure to read the entire policy. Some will say we don't sell your information anymore, BUT we are going to group all of your data in a demographic and share that with advertisers.
- ☑ What information on your device they will look at, such as the device's unique ID, operating system, browser type and history, IP address, event stamp, and error logs? After reading the privacy policies, many of them state they will collect information about the tech near your devices, like Bluetooth-enabled devices, wifi access points, and cell towers. How many houses have family members that each have a smartphone, laptop, or desktop that have blue tooth turned on?  Don't forget how many smart devices could be in your home, including

personal AI assistant devices, smart TVs, sound bars,
appliances, your vehicles, and game systems. We really
don't want an app snooping around other devices in our
homes and taking information from them.

☑ Many of the policies say they will share your information
with another organization if they are legally required to do
it, OR they may give it to researchers.  Yikes!!!!!!!  Are
you kidding me?!" They did not say who the researchers
were. Be very careful with whom you share and connect
your digital information; they may have ulterior motives.
Once you click, you legally agree to them.

☑ How their app or website protects your data.  One policy
we read said that people in the EU, UK, Canada,
Australia, New Zealand, and California have some
additional rights with their data.  You are going to see
more and more of this in the future with digital privacy
rights.

☑ One policy we looked at gave details of where they
"SHARE" your personal information, including a drop-
down menu to click on whom you give them permission
to share your data.  Remember, no one is in business to
give something away for free.

☑ One policy stated they can copyright content used with
their service.  That means the data you put on their app
belongs to that company. Another app's privacy policy

stated they have exclusive rights to use and publish the content in any media. That should be concerning.

- ☑ Many of the apps will talk about what happens if you take them to court.  It is common to see language stating that if you go to court over a dispute, you both are waive the right to a trial by jury.

- ☑ One site said that they share your information only **where reasonably necessary.**  We don't know about you, but what someone else views as necessary may not be what we view as necessary.  Keep in mind, many companies put a clause in that they can share all your data with any company that they buy or merge with. The merged companies may have completely different data policies than the one you originally agreed to.

- ☑ One app said we have partners that want to sell you ads, and we will share your information with them.  Also, those partners will tell us about you, and we will be collecting that information.

- ☑ Apps can also collect your precise location and location to the place of service.

- ☑ Apps can collect personal information like your race, gender, religious beliefs, biometrics, and political opinions.  This concerns us, especially with we think of the importance of democracy, privacy, and freedom.

- ☑ App privacy policies are nice enough to let you know they will access your contacts, emails, texts, photos, and audio files. If you post a photo, you have been given access to your photos.  If you post a video on your phone, you have been given access to your microphone.
- ☑ We saved the best for last. We were reading the privacy policy of an app that said it would record your health and financial information, and if they need to, can get your credit score.

## Is Data Privacy a Choice?

You should cherish your privacy and freedoms. We have spoken with folks that are younger than us to hear their perspective.  I am told that in many cases, you have to accept what the tech company is offering because you need the service they are offering in your city, society, culture, job, or social group to stay connected and engaged.

We really do understand this position. We, too, love the conveniences of technology.  When we travel for business, we use our phones to basically interact with the town where we are visiting, from catching cabs to figuring out where to eat, to checking on our flight when we are leaving the town. However, if we keep giving companies more and more information about us and submitting to their rules to simply exist, we are in essence, giving people and technology too much control of our life.

To us, privacy is incredibly important.

(Jimmy speaking) The America I love is all about individual choice, freedom, and the ability to pursue your dreams. While talking to my mom and dad I shared the impact "1984" and "Animal Farm" had on me when I read them in high school. These books, along with having a family that fought in the military to protect personal freedoms, have sunk deep into my psyche. The big question is, are we giving away our freedoms for digital convenience?  If we are going to continue to participate in the digital world, we must learn how to safeguard our privacy as much as possible. Let's take a closer look at what lawmakers are doing and why.

**Privacy Legislation**

California has been a leader in digital privacy laws.  An excerpt from Assembly Bill No. 375, chapter 55 states,

"Beginning January 1, 2020, the bill would grant a consumer a right to request a business to disclose the categories and specific pieces of personal information that it collects about the consumer, the categories of sources from which that information is collected, the business purposes for collecting or selling the information, and the categories of 3rd parties with which the information is shared. The bill would require a business to make disclosures about the information and the purposes for which it is used. The bill would grant a consumer the right to request the deletion of personal information and would require the business to delete it upon receipt of a verified request, as specified. The bill would grant a consumer a right to request that a business that sells the consumer's personal information or discloses it for a business purpose disclose the categories of information that it collects and categories of information and the identity of 3rd parties to which the information was sold or disclosed. The bill would require a business to provide this information in response to a verifiable consumer request. The bill would authorize a consumer to opt-out of the sale of personal information by a business and would prohibit the business from discriminating against the consumer for exercising this right, including by charging the consumer who opts out a different price or providing the consumer a different quality of goods or services, except if the difference is reasonably related to the value provided by the consumer's data."

We live in California and appreciate the option to say to businesses, you don't have my permission to sell my data. However, there are companies that make this case that they don't really SELL your personal data but use your data for people who are advertising with them. Some of the advice that has been past down to me is that if it walks like a duck, quacks like a duck, and swims like a duck, chances are it is a duck. Our opinion is that we have folks saying I am not a duck, but they really are ducks.

After the California Consumer Privacy Act was passed, many states began looking into digital privacy laws. There is a "US State Privacy Legislation Tracker" by iapp.org (13) where you can track what is happening with your state's privacy laws. At the time of publishing this book, five states have signed into legislation bills.

**Your Friendly Neighborhood Data Broker**

The US Federal Trade Commission identifies data brokers as "companies that collect consumers' personal information and resell or share that information with others—are

important participants in this Big Data economy." https://
www.ftc.gov/system/files/documents/reports/data-brokers-
call-transparency-accountability-report-federal-trade-
commission-may-2014/140527databrokerreport.pdf (14).

**Senators Ask . . .**

In April of 2021, a group of US Senators sent a letter to
AT&T, Index Exchange, Google, Magnite, OpenX, PubMatic,
Twitter, and Verizon and asked the following questions (from
a press release from warner.senate.gov)
"1. Please identify the specific data elements about users,
their devices, the websites they are accessing, and the apps
they are using that you provide to auction participants.
2. Please identify each company, foreign or domestic, to
whom your firm has provided bidstream data in the past
three years that is not contractually prohibited from sharing,
selling, or using the data for any purpose unrelated to
bidding on and delivering an ad.
3. If your firm has contractual restrictions in place prohibiting
the sharing, sale, or secondary use of bidstream data,
please detail all efforts to audit compliance with these
contractual restrictions and the results of those audits.
4. Please identify each foreign-headquartered or foreign-
majority-owned company to whom your firm has provided

bidstream data from users in the United States and their devices in the past three years."

The press release went on to say that the "The senators are seeking information about the sharing of Americans' data through 'real time bidding' – the auction process used to place many targeted digital advertisements. For most online ads, although only one company wins the auction, hundreds of firms participating receive information about the potential recipient of the ad, including device identifiers and cookies, web browsing and location data, IP addresses, and age and gender.

Few Americans realize that some auction participants are siphoning off and storing 'bidstream' data to compile exhaustive dossiers about them. In turn, these dossiers are being openly sold to anyone with a credit card, including to hedge funds, political campaigns, and even to governments, the senators wrote." The press release from Senator Warn's website went on to say that "This information would be a goldmine for foreign intelligence services that could exploit it to inform and supercharge hacking, blackmail, and influence campaigns."

**Last Word on Privacy**

When your personal privacy is seen as a commodity that companies profit from, it is time to really start evaluating what you are sacrificing for the ease and comfort of using your mobile device. In America (where we live), freedom and privacy are values instilled in our culture. We both come from a long line of patriots who value one's freedom and right to have a private life.

That being said, in today's world, you may have to participate in a technology community that does not give you a great deal of choice in privacy.  There are several lawsuits involving education organizations or corporations mandating that their employees and students upload their private health information into a third-party provider's app on their phone to share their vaccination status. Many people are concerned about the safety and privacy of their health information.

In America, we value privacy. Consider the following areas:
- HIPPA protects our health information.
- The 1st amendment gives us privacy in our religious choices.  Something we hold very dear to our hearts.
- The 3rd amendment says we don't have to house soldiers in the privacy of my home.

- The 4th amendment protects our privacy, and prevents unlawful searches and seizures on our homes.

- The 5th amendment says that the government cannot force us testify against ourselves. We have all heard on tv, "I plead the 5th." However, can you plead the 5th if companies are searching and sharing your data against your knowledge?

- The 9th amendment states, "enumeration in the Constitution of certain rights shall not be construed to deny or disparage other rights retained by the people." Some legal scholars view this as the right to have personal privacy. However, like many Americans, when social media began, we clicked away privacy to simply participate in something that was new and exciting.

**Stopping Unwanted Visitors from Accessing your Devices**

Here are a few ideas to stop unwanted visitors from accessing your devices.

(1) Turn your router off at night or when you are not using it. The simple fact is that while you are sleeping, turning off your wifi prevents access to you or your devices.

(2) Turn your Bluetooth off and only use it when absolutely
necessary.

(3) Go to the privacy settings of your device and go through
everything and get an understanding of who and what is
asking for access to your information.

(4) Check your mic and camera, to make sure you have not
given someone permission to listen to you and look at
your photos.

(5) If you must have your phone on at night, put it in airplane
mode.

(6) When you travel or are in public, consider putting your
phone in a Faraday bag.

(7)  Turn off Wifi when not using it.

(8)  Remove apps you have not used in a while.

(9)  Use two factor authentication whenever possible.

(10)  Update your operating system.

(11)  Avoid public charging stations.

(12)  Use built-in device protections like Find My…

(13)  Don't overshare on social media.

(14)  Use Anti/Malware/AntiVirus apps.


**Social Engineering First Aid Kit**


We would imagine that if we were over at your home and
you accidentally cut your finger, that most of you would have

band-aids, aspirin, and ointment to stop the cut from getting infected.  You can pretty much go to any store and get a first aid kit that has these things in them.  The idea is that if a small injury happens, you can take care of it. But what happens when an attack happens in the digital environment of your house or car?  Let's start pulling together your social engineering first aid kit. We will discuss Browsers, Data Mining, VPNs, blocking unwanted calls, secure texting, and other tactics to help you protect yourself.

**Browsers**

There are more and more news stories in the press talking about multi-factor authentication (MFA) attacks that happen in browsers. Many people work remotely and use browsers to perform the functions of their job. Here is an interesting read on the Uber breach entitled "Multi-Factor Authentication Fatigue Key Factor in Uber Breach" at https://www.infoq.com/news/2022/09/Uber-breach-mfa-fatigue/.

There are programs available to help keep your data safe when using a browser. For example, Privacy Badger will learn and block invisible trackers created by the Electronic

Frontier Foundation (EFF) https://privacybadger.org/ (15), NoScript https://noscript.net/  (16) helps you stay safe in your browser and protects against clickjacking https://owasp.org/www-community/attacks/Clickjacking (17), and Cross Site Scripting XSS https://owasp.org/www-community/attacks/xss/  (18), can be added as an extension in Firefox.

## Targeted Ads and Data Mining

We have talked in this book about why people want your data. When you think of data mining, think of workers going to the side of a mountain to look for coal or gold.  The idea is that you go to an area and chip away until you find something that is valuable.

Today, companies use all the data collected to identify patterns on where people go and what they buy.  There was a story a few years ago about a man in Minnesota who got upset with Target because they were sending his teenage daughter coupons for baby clothes. Irate, the father called the company to complain. Little did he know his daughter actually was pregnant, and the customer tracking technology Target employed was so precise it was able to predict an early pregnancy simply based on the items his daughter searched for online. https://observer.com/2016/07/the-truth-about-data-mining-how-online-trackers-gather-your-info-and-what-they-see/ (19). Browser History and Cookies play a major role in this data mining. When a user visits a site with an advertiser's cookie embedded, it makes a request to other sites to share information. This is called Cookie syncing. Once two or more trackers sync cookies, they're able to exchange specific user data between their individual servers, enabling them to paint a much more accurate picture of who you are and what you may be interested in. Changing your browser's individual cookie policy to block outside sources, disabling Flash on your computer, installing Chrome anti-tracking browser extensions like uBlock Origin https://www.expressvpn.com/blog/the-3-best-browser-extensions-to-protect-your-privacy/ (20), and using a virtual private network (VPN) can help keep your identity hidden while protecting your information.

**VPN**

What is a virtual private network? Think of a VPN as a tunnel or hallway that connects you and your device to the internet. This tunnel has security built into it so folks can see what you are up to.  There are a number of products on the market.  I would pause reading the book here and purchase a VPN product for your devices.

**Unwanted Texts and Phone Calls**

If you get constant unwanted phone calls, there are a few things you can do:
1.  Block the contact
2.  Report the number to your carrier by texting the number to 7726. This works for most cell phone carriers.
3.  Use your provider's spam detector to help protect you from unwanted phone calls and texts

**Secure Texting**

We love secured texting.  When we attend cyber events, we will have our team use a secured texting application. Why? You might ask. So our activity can't be monitored by an outside person or business. There is a risk that hackers can get access to your information and monitor it directly though texting.  Secure texting Apps provide end-to-end encryption that is secure. Signal or Wire are examples of Secure Texting Apps. Our native Apps like Facebook Messenger and Apple Message or Android Messages are not secure and do not use end-to-end encryption. Please, when communicating confidential information via Text message, use a secure text app.

**Must-Watch Videos on Social Engineering!**

- Watch Rachel Tobac live "How Would I Hack You?" at: https://go.dashlane.com/How-Would-I-Hack-You.html (21).
- Here is another Rachel Video from KringleCon https://www.youtube.com/watch?v=L5J2PgGOLtE (22)
- Watch Alethe Denis " Burn Notice: Confronting an Online Scammer"! https://www.youtube.com/watch?v=3U8w58022TA (23)
- Another video with Alethe: https://www.cnn.com/videos/business/2022/10/18/donie-osullivan-hacked-defcon-contd-orig-gr-jm.cnn (24).

**Social Profiles**

Be careful about what you put on your socials and who sees it. Take some time and go through your family's social profiles and really have a talk about what you are putting out there and who is looking. We mentioned a video earlier in the book with Jack Dorsey and the Social Media Experiment. After watching it, think about what a stranger can learn about you on your social profile.

**Catfishing**

Earlier in the book, we shared with you how someone can create a fake persona. Catfishing is when someone uses a fake persona on social media or dating websites to get money, control, or information from you.

Once a connection is made online, be on alert if it seems like too much too fast.  Remember, someone can't love you or be a soul mate after a week.

Here are some things to be aware of to avoid getting catfished:

(1) If they ask for money, RUN!!!! Don't give it to them.

(2) If they are asking you to do things like video yourself.

(3) If they demand to only communicate on certain messaging platforms and refuse to do a live video.

(4) If their social account has not been around long and they don't have a great deal of engagement.

(5) Do a background check on the person.  Make sure they are who they say they are.

(6) Don't give away your personal information.

(7) Use common sense.  If something doesn't seem right about their profile and pictures, listen to yourself.  A healthy dose of being a little paranoid is a good thing.

## USB Blocker

We have all been guilty of this one; whether we are in a hotel room, rental car, or other public places, we will plug our phones into just about anything to keep them charged.

Just like your mom told you not to take candy from strangers, the same applies to your phone.  Don't plug your device into an unknown USB source.  You may want to add a USB blocker to your social engineering first aid kit. The USB blocker will stop unwanted data access of your information in a public port. It is pretty simple how this works. The USB blocker will plug into a port, and then you plug your device into the USB blocker.

Read what a (25) credit card skimmer is and what you can do to be safe! We also use (26) the new product to secure you from NFC scams. The Hunter Cat (27) detects malicious card readers that are placed over the top of a legitimate credit card reader. The Hunter Cat allows someone to test and look for credit card skimmers. You can use a Hunter Cat while accessing public credit card places.  The other day, (Henry) I stopped in my local gas station, and low and behold, the gas pump had been hacked and had a credit card skimmer attached and was illegally stealing credit card data.

## Protecting kids

We have an entire chapter dedicated to protecting children. The takeaway from digital dust is that you need to be aware of whom your kids interact with online and what messaging apps they use.  You also want to teach your kids (of all ages) how to protect themselves in the digital world. We will detail more of this in the Digital Defense and Social Martial Arts chapter.

## Car with stickers

You know the minivan I am talking about. You pull up a stop light, and the minivan in front of you tells you a great deal about the people inside.  You ask how? Let's look at all the information on the back of the van:

(1)  The stick figures of their family with everyone's name.
(2)  Stickers that tell us about your honor roll student and where they go to school.
(3)  Political affiliations.
(4)  Sports teams their kids play on.
(5)  Favorite vacation spots.

(6)  Personalize the tag with your name (maybe even their passcode).

(7)  The name of your pets.

(8)  Information about their or their spouses' profession.

Please take a few minutes and read what a local police department came up with at https://www.wsls.com/news/local/2020/09/03/how-the-bedford-police-department-says-you-could-be-oversharing-through-bumper-stickers/ (28).

Your well-intention stickers and license plate may be considered valuable by a predator because that allows them to learn a great deal about your family, where you live, where the kids go to school, and what kind of activities they kids do, and who your pets are.

# What information are you DRIVING around?

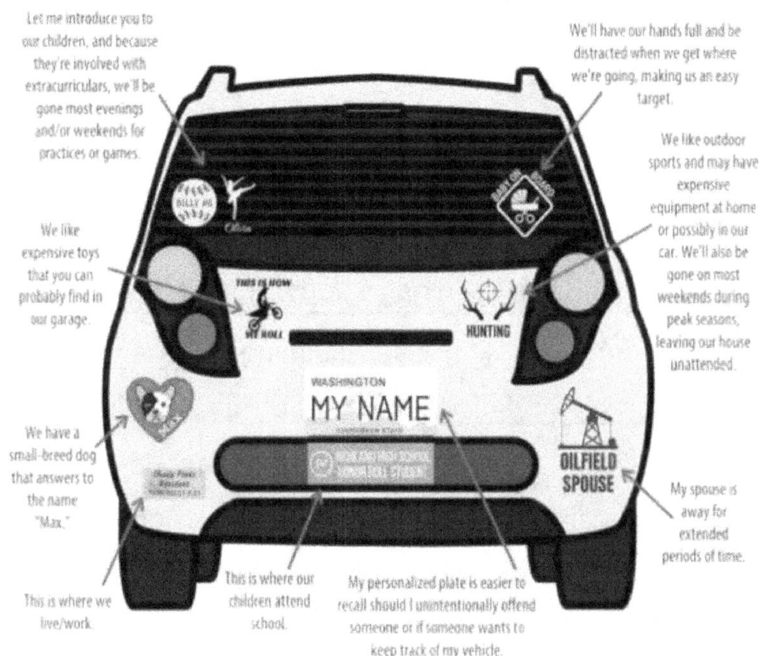



**Source: Bedford, Virginia Police Department Facebook Page. August 19, 2020**

**Be safe in Hotels AirBnBs when Traveling | Cameras may be Present!**

Marcus Hutchins, a famous hacker who stopped WannaCry posts, shares interesting tactics to help everyone be safe. Warning: before reading and watching the following links, staying at hotels and other rentals may never be the same. Proceed with caution. This article: https://www.techtimes.com/articles/265013/20210905/how-to-spot-airbnb-hidden-cameras-tiktok-user-claiming-to-be-an-ex-hacker-exposes-on-viral-video.htm (29) discusses how to use a mobile phone flashlight to check for nefarious cameras. Here is another video from his TikTok account https://www.tiktok.com/@malwaretech/video/7002804220126661893?lang=en (30).

### Digital Dust Wrap Up

There is a great deal of information in here that is designed to protect you. The bottom line is that you omit digital dust when you interact with the digital world. We encourage you to take the time and start using the tactics described in this chapter to protect yourself and your family.

## Website References

We realize there are many ways and styles to cite web references. We think the easiest way is to just copy and select the URL into your browser. This book was written over two years.  Please note that we don't have control if the content and links change over time.

(1) https://emfacademy.com/check-sar-value-mobile-phone/

(2) https://www.apple.com/legal/rfexposure/

(3) https://www.lg.com/global/support/sar/sar

(4) https://rfhealth-sar.motorola.com/SAR/

(5) https://www.samsung.com/sar/sarMain.do

(6) https://blog.red-website-design.co.uk/2022/09/07/social-trends-finish-with-bang/

(7) https://www.linkedin.com/pulse/what-digital-dust-should-we-worry-ours-ema-linaker/

(8) https://www.gartner.com/en/newsroom/press-releases/2020-10-19-gartner-identifies-the-top-strategic-technology-trends-for-2021

(9) https://webkay.robinlinus.com/

(10)  https://www.allaboutcookies.org/mobile/index.html

(11) https://www.adjust.com/glossary/idfv/

(12) https://youtu.be/YgKz_KLE_yk

(13) iapp.org

(14) https://www.ftc.gov/system/files/documents/reports/
data-brokers-call-transparency-accountability-report-federal-
trade-commission-may-2014/140527databrokerreport.pdf

(15) https://privacybadger.org/

(16) https://noscript.net/

(17) https://owasp.org/www-community/attacks/Clickjacking

(18) https://owasp.org/www-community/attacks/xss/

(19) https://observer.com/2016/07/the-truth-about-data-
mining-how-online-trackers-gather-your-info-and-what-they-
see/

(20) https://www.expressvpn.com/blog/the-3-best-browser-
extensions-to-protect-your-privacy/

(21) https://go.dashlane.com/How-Would-I-Hack-You.html

(22) https://www.youtube.com/watch?v=L5J2PgGOLtE(25)

(23) https://www.youtube.com/watch?v=3U8w58022TA

(24) https://www.cnn.com/videos/business/2022/10/18/donie-
osullivan-hacked-defcon-contd-orig-gr-jm.cnn

(25) https://www.pcmag.com/how-to/how-to-spot-and-avoid-
credit-card-skimmers

(26) https://electroniccats.com/store/hunter-cat-nfc/

(27) https://electroniccats.com/store/huntercat/

(28) https://www.wsls.com/news/local/2020/09/03/how-the-bedford-police-department-says-you-could-be-oversharing-through-bumper-stickers/

(29) https://www.techtimes.com/articles/265013/20210905/how-to-spot-airbnb-hidden-cameras-tiktok-user-claiming-to-be-an-ex-hacker-exposes-on-viral-video.htm

(30) https://www.tiktok.com/@malwaretech/video/7002804220126661893?lang=en

(31) https://learn.snhu.edu/d2l/lor/viewer/viewFile.d2lfile/760194/22533,-1/

# NOTES

# Chapter 6
# DIGITAL DEFENSE AND SOCIAL MARTIAL ARTS

Welcome to your first lesson in digital defense and social martial arts. Many of us have had the opportunity to participate in martial arts or boxing training. We both have had the opportunity to train and have immense respect for martial arts.  We grew up watching martial arts on TV and in the movies.

For those of you who have not had the experience of taking a martial arts class, one of the basic techniques you learn is how to block a punch and kick.  No matter what your technical skill is, we are going to show everyone from Generation Z to Baby Boomers techniques to stop, block, and defend themselves from anyone trying to digitally attack you.

**"It is not the size of the dog in the fight, but the size of the fight in the dog." Mark Twain**

In the last chapter, we shared what to have in your first aid kit, but now it is time to hit the mats and learn some digital defense.

We have always loved the story of an underdog taking on the big bully and prevailing. One of our favorite books is Malcolm Gladwell's "David and Goliath, Underdogs, Misfits, and the Art of Battling Giants." The story of David and Goliath is about an underdog kicking the butt of the bully. I highly suggest you read the story in Gladwell's book.

The cybercrime we talk about in this book can seem overwhelming when thinking about how to stand up to these Goliath types of hackers. We will teach you offensive and defensive strategies to combat cyber criminals in later chapters.

If you are not familiar with the story, let me give you a few highlights:

- **PLAYERS:** The Israelites and the Philistines were fighting. Goliath was team Philistine, and David was Team Israel.
- **CHALLENGE:** Goliath challenged the Israelite Army saying, "Choose a man and have him come down to

me. If he is able to fight and kill me, we will become your subjects; but if I overcome him and kill him, you will become our subjects and serve us."

- **BIG DOG - LITTLE DOG:** Goliath was big; David was not. Most texts I have read believe that Goliath was somewhere between 6'9" and 9' and David was between 5' and 5'4".
- **BATTLE WEAPONS BIG DOG:** Goliath had the state-of-art of equipment of the day. He had a bronze helmet, upper body and leg armor, and a fighting spear. He even had a shield bearer who walked in front of him to protect him.
- **BATTLE WEAPONS LITTLE DOG:** Faith, confidence, speed, and stones.
- **FINAL SCORE:** David Wins!

Gladwell makes the point in his book that the stone slung by David had the power equivalent to a .45 caliber pistol. Now Goliath was huge, and many believe he had acromegaly. Acromegaly is a medical issue where one's pituitary glands make too much growth hormone. One side effect of this is problems with your eyesight. David did not fight Goliath in a traditional battle with big spears and shields. David started running at Goliath. Old Goliath, with his poor eyesight, probably could not track David's quick movements. David slung a stone and hit Goliath smack in the middle of his forehead, killing him instantly.

**So what is the point of this?**

You may think you can't fight a big cyberbully or social engineer, but don't underestimate yourself. Caring for your family, friends, and coworkers brings a lot to any fight.  You bought a book on how to protect yourself.  So let's get ready to learn how to use social martial arts to block and kick.

(Jimmy ) I learned many lessons while training in Hwardo under Grand Master Kwon. Grand Master Kwon was truly a badass and one of the most graceful human beings I have ever met. He had a code of respect that he lived by, and his students were expected to do the same.

One of the best lessons Grand Master Kwon taught me was not to underestimate your opponent. During one of our classes, Grand Master bought me up in front of the class. I was easily a full head taller than him and was physically a much bigger man.  Kwon told me to try to hit him.  Within a second, he blocked my punch, grabbed my other hand, and bent it back, putting me on my knees.  It really hurt.  Grand

Master Kwon showed the class that knowing how to block in any fight is critical. So, your first lesson is blocking.

**Blocking**

Blocking is one of the first things you need to learn in digital defense. We are going to teach you how to block using a 3-step digital technique that will include:

- Validating then trust
- Double checking data
- Knowing who gets physical access to your work and home

**Validation and Digital Blocking**

We have shared with you countless scams and sources to get information.  Let's break each of the points down a little more. When you are first contacted by someone, validate that the person sending you the information is legit.  Who are they, and why are they sending you information?

The other day, I got a notice to update a password for an application that I was not familiar with. It kept coming up even when I canceled it. I took a screenshot of the message and called technical support.  Tech support validated the message and explained to me what it was and why my computer was having this issue.

If you don't know the person, try to validate who they are. We have talked at length about how a social engineer will put pressure on you to do something, and in previous chapters we provided you with some clues to figure out if a person's online presence is fake.

Once I received an email from my email hosting company saying it was time to either update the password or keep the old one. The email looked authentic, including logos.  So, as a digital defense master, I rolled over (not clicked) the link and looked at the URL.  It was a trap!  The URL listed was https://india.youthicon.net/ (the name of my email provider).

Here is a resource to check on questionable/nefarious websites:  https://payback-ltd.com/blogs/12-easy-ways-to-check-if-a-website-is-legit-or-a-scam/ (1)
and two websites you can use to check to see if a website is not nefarious:  https://www.virustotal.com/gui/home/upload VirusTotal (2)  https://www.urlvoid.com/ Urlvoid (3).

Let me share one more example. I recently received a text from my niece's school asking to donate to a fundraiser.  As a digital defense master, I deleted the message. The next time I spoke with my sister, I shared that she should let the school know folks are doing this. It ended up it was a true fundraiser.  Always validate!

In the event that the person is physically coming at you rather than digitally, you should have a list of who is allowed on the premises at your office and home. Now we are older, but even in the 70s and 80s, our parents had a passcode set up that they would give someone if we needed to be picked up in case of an emergency.  For example, if kids were at home, and someone randomly came to the door saying come with me, your mom and dad said to take you to the hospital because they were in a crash.  The response should be what's the passcode? If they didn't know the passcode, the kids were to slam the door shut, lock it,  and call the cops.

We shared a few stories in the book about how we accessed different physical environments and ways we were stopped or not stopped.  If it is at your workplace, the same rules apply. You should know who is allowed to have physical access to your facility.  If someone unfamiliar comes, validate and check out their story.  The point is that you can block people by double-checking who they are and what they want.  If the story does not check out, you have thwarted an unwanted visitor.

You Just Passed Blocking 101; now let's jump into other blocking techniques.

**Privacy settings for your computer, phone, car, business, apps, and house.**

We imagine that most of you check the doors and windows of your home and cars every night before you go to bed to protect yourself and your belongings. Do you do this with your tech?

We also imagine that most of you, whether you are in the office or at home, have a laptop or desktop computer, smartphone, and possibly a pad or tablet device.  You may also have smart devices and gaming systems that can connect to your phone and computer through Bluetooth. Each of these devices has security settings.

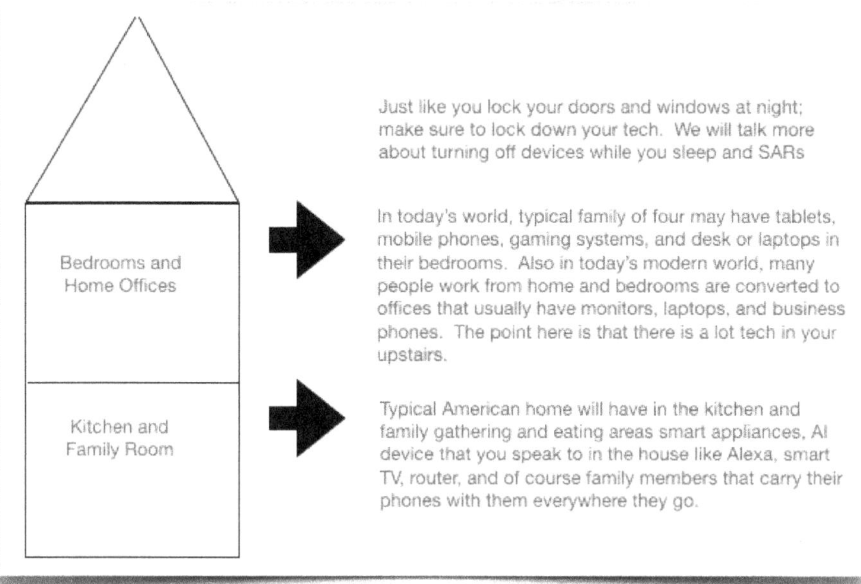



Let's start with always updating your router settings and firmware! We really encourage you to stop reading the book and look at all of your devices' security settings.

When we first started doing this, we could not believe all the people that unassumingly allowed access to our mic, camera, and photos. Don't forget to look at your tracking and privacy settings. You may have inadvertently given people permission to track your activity and your location on your devices.

Go through each app on your phone and see what settings are checked.  Many times we click accept when downloading an app, and we agree to things we really should not.  If you have children, no matter the age, go through this with them on their phones.  The same goes for computers and tablets. One of the best ways to block cyber criminals is to make sure your privacy settings are not giving people access to your personal information.  Whenever we teach a course on digital defense, there are always people in the audience that are just blown away by who and what is monitoring and tracking them.

Think of your home as an electronic martial arts practice arena that you need to protect. First and foremost, set a new password on your home router and use best practices when creating a passphrase. Use a free service like LastPass password generator https://www.lastpass.com/features/password-generator (4). Second, update ALL devices to the latest firmware. Routers are consumables that are meant to work for 3-4 years. Companies stop updating the firmware, and the router becomes obsolete and unsafe. Physical entry can also be a concern. Use upgraded locks like Abloy's Deadbolt https://securitysnobs.com/Abloy/ (5). Wifi access can be used to gain access to devices in your home, and criminals may steal your personally identifiable information.

Always use WPA3 or the latest encryption your router offers. GET a new/updated router with the latest firmware every few years. These are consumables and need to be replaced. Set up protections to protect your family. Check physical entry access like doors, windows, and your electronic footprint, meaning Routers, BlueTooth devices, and Internet of Things (IoT) devices. Ensure all are secure.

**Dangers of Public Wifi:**

Watch this video on The Dangers of Public Wi-Fi https://www.youtube.com/watch?v=vz9IPVhBUpc (6). Always be careful of using Public Available Wi-Fi networks. A SSIDs or (Service Set Identifier) is the name of a Wi-Fi network. For example, at your house, your home network may be called "home." Sometimes hackers will mimic SSIDs (the router's name) to trick you into thinking you are on a legitimate network when in reality, they use it to steal your data!

**Let's work on a few more blocking techniques.**

Turn off your router at night.  There are both health reasons as well as technical reasons to do this. Does the internet really need to be running while you are sleeping? Take a look at how many of your neighbor's wifi are available to access at different times of the night. Bad actors may strike at night when people are sleeping.

This next blocking technique was really hard for us to discipline ourselves on, but we're hitting about 90% on this; turn your Bluetooth off.  Before we lecture you on the why, let's discuss how much we love Bluetooth.  There are many cool gadgets that we can connect to our tech.  The problem is that we are vulnerable when we have our Bluetooth connection on. We talked about this in earlier chapters. If you are not using it, turn it off. One time as a passenger in a call, I did a Bluetooth search of all the people driving by me. All you need is to connect with one vulnerable person to get access to their phone or vehicle's settings and information.

The other blocking technique we mentioned earlier includes keeping your devices, credit cards with chips, and Key FOB (Free on Board) in a Faraday bag when you travel or are in public. These attacks are less likely today because threat actors no longer need to get close to a victim to steal their information. They are now able to access the endless list of compromised credit cards available on the dark web! It is still important to be vigilant. Similar to the Faraday bag, we suggest always using a layer of tinfoil to wrap your vehicle's

Remote Key FOB (Free on Board ) at home or while traveling. While you may want to keep your passport in a Faraday bag for extra protection, passport covers already contain RFID-blocking material. Passports can only be scanned if they are wide open.

We think that is enough on blocking.  By the way, I just doubled check my phone, and my Bluetooth was on.  I am taking my own advice and turning it off now!

**Digital Kicking**

You can only block so long; sometimes, you have to kick. Back in the day, I (Jimmy) had quite a mouth on me. I recall one summer evening, I rode my BMX to 7-11 to drink Slurpees and play Pac-Man.  And yes, in true 80's fashion, my hair was parted in the middle and feathered back. I also sported a pair of Clyde Drexler Pumas and lots of 80's swagger!  Long story short, I got into it with some dudes at 7-11. When I walked out to get on my killer BMX, one of the two guys had I mouthed off to grabbed me off my bike by putting a chain around my neck.  My reaction was to grab the chain. However, the other guy started hitting me in the stomach.  I was outnumbered. However, an opportunity presented itself where I could kick the guy that was hitting me in the stomach.  Actually, when I tried to kick him, my Puma flew off and hit him in the face.  This gave me a quick second to pull the other guy off me and make a run for it. My point here is that when you are fighting digitally, you may have to kick. We do not promote violence or harassment in any situation.

So let's look at how you can digitally kick a hacker or stop a social engineer. One way to use your social martial arts is by asking questions that slow down your attacker. When approached by a stranger, be cautious and on your toes. Ask them the who, what, where, and why questions. Attackers will want to glean information from you. Be very careful about what you share. These questions will help slow down the hacker and the attack, and maybe the hacker will move along. Another is learning about the many attacks social engineers use to gain information and use it against you. We have discussed many of these attacks, including Phishing, Smishing, Tailgating, and others. Another sidekick you can give to Social Engineer tactics isby using 2FA (two-factor authentication) when it is available. Social Engineers prey on urgency and hope you can be tricked. Be mindful of risks, double-check, triple-check any request, and do your own research! Quick Kick tip- reverse lookup a phone # see if the rest of the planet has received that spam call!

Here is a link to a WIRED story that highlights a phone scam and uses personal finance apps to exploit people https://www.wired.com/story/phone-scam-phishing-finance-apps/ (7). Remember, phone scams are a type of social engineering tactic, and user education is one way to bypass these attacks. When contacted by phone, one digital defense tactic is to get their number and call them back. Before calling back, do a reverse phone lookup to see if this may be a scam. To further understand, here is an article on a month in the life of a social engineer https://www.itpro.com/security/social-engineering/361911/month-in-the-life-of-social-engineer-week-one (8).


**Roundhouse Kick**

You are ready to come full circle and learn one of the most complex and powerful attacks, the roundhouse kick. Let's look at how to deal with this from a full-circle perspective, step-by-step. Social engineering roundhouse kicks will help protect you.

The more data or information social engineers have on a target, the more successful they will be in gaining your trust and tricking you. you can protect yourself by limiting what you share online, including your location. You don't need your GPS on, allowing others to see where you are at all times. Only share vacation photos after, not during the holiday travels. Use skepticism and be ready for online and in-person attacks. Use other methods of communication to trust/verify that a message is legitimate. This CompTIA article https://www.comptia.org/content/articles/anatomy-of-a-social-engineering-attack (9) explains in detail how to avoid social engineering attacks. You can also take a look at https://comptiacdn.azureedge.net/webcontent/docs/default-source/research-reports/avoid-social-engineering-attacks.pdf?sfvrsn=28ea7377_2 (10).

**So you can digitally kick and block, now what?**

We grew up in the era of Chuck Norris, Bruce Lee, Gymkata, Karate Kid, and tons of other really cool karate movies.  As kids, we were obsessed with martial arts weapons as much as the physical practice itself.

There are digital weapons that you can put into your arsenal to help you fight and protect yourself.

- Software - There are many software solutions you can get for your phones and computers to protect you against attacks. We use antivirus / antimalware on our laptops and personal computers, but we should also use them on our mobile devices. Here are three we have reviewed and have 4 stars- Malwarebytes Mobile Security, Sophos Intercept X for Mobile, & Trend Micro Mobile Security Password Protection.

- Passcodes- The passcode to your phone is also a weapon against being hacked. Always use a passcode to protect anyone from gaining access to your phone if you lose it or you are away from the device.  (Remember to please use caution and think before you click when you are on your mobile device.)

- Passwords- Passwords can be cracked. Frequently changing passwords and enabling 2FA or dual-factor authentication is a must! The use of a password manager is highly recommended. In order to circumvent hackers, one must always add more layers to protect themselves. Creating complex passwords is part of the process. The more layers you add, like 2FA or OTP, the safer you are in the long run.

Never reuse passwords; always create new unique passwords/passphrases; and never use personal information in your passwords! The amount of password breaches is enormous, and those breached passwords have been added to a large database on the Darkweb. In 2021, the largest password compilation of all time RockYou2021, was leaked online with 8.4 billion entries! https://cybernews.com/security/rockyou2021-alltime-largest-password-compilation-leaked/ (11). If you would like to learn more about the world's biggest breaches and hacks, take a look at this link:   https://www.informationisbeautiful.net/visualizations/worlds-biggest-data-breaches-hacks/ (12).

Here is a list of the most common passwords/top 500 https://www.informationisbeautiful.net/visualizations/top-500-passwords-visualized/  (13). Are yours on there? Has your email has been breached? https://haveibeenpwned.com/ (14).

Do you know the most used password in the world?  If you guessed 123456, you are right.  Other popular choices are "password" or number sequences like 111111 or 123456789.  Don't make your passwords predictable or easy for anyone to guess. For all your passwords, we suggest using both upper and lower-case letters, numbers, and symbols. It helps not to have words and phrases that are related.  For example, if you went to the University of Maryland like me, don't use "go terps" as your passcode.  If you have certain images or phrases on your social media, don't use them as a passcode.

- Security Extensions- Another tip is to use security extensions and plugins to help you become more secure. Here are a few to check out in this article https://www.sysprobs.com/best-chrome-security-extensions (15).

- Reverse phone number search- Use a free reverse phone lookup website. Take a look at this article at https://www.sfweekly.com/sponsored/completely-free-reverse-phone-lookup-with-name/ (16) discussing this.

- Secure browsers- Secure browsers can block sharing of your data. We suggest your try Brave, Firefox Focus, or Duck Duck Go. You can use Ad blockers as well!

- VPNs- VPN stands for virtual private network. Putting VPN software on your phone and computer can be a lifesaver.  When you look at the internet through a VPN, it encrypts both your connection and what you are looking at so that people cannot track you. We are big fans of tunnel bear, but there are other products on the market too.  For less than what it costs to get your car's oil changed, you can subscribe and get a VPN solution. Look at it like a VPN as an UNDERGROUND Road as opposed to the normal roads you travel daily. VPN keeps you and your information encrypted and safe from hackers' eyes.

- Old Tech - There are many places that ask you to donate your old technology so that it can be recycled and repurposed. Before you donate or give your old tech, make sure you have deleted *everything*.  The same goes for fax machines and copiers. Many times people leave important, private information on their computers like social security numbers, financial information, health care records, and other personal information about you and your family.  IRS.gov has a table on how to get rid of old floppy files and CDs. Older technology needs to be destroyed either physically or digitally. Physically, meaning destroy using safe methods, a hammer or scissors, and safety gear. Digitally, meaning using a secure method to wipe all data from the hard drive. Macs and PCs have this capability, and there is third-party software available to do this.  Ensure you have a shredder at your home to destroy private information.

Thieves still dumpster dive and can collect data that may harm you in the future.

I know you are exhausted, but we must press on padawan (for all you Star Wars Fans). Your training is not complete. This next move is a really important one for you to master and teach your family, community, and employees. So what is the name of this next move?

## "Sayonara" Social Blocking

Sayonara means goodbye or farewell. For many of us that are on social media, we are accustomed to connecting with people and accepting new acquaintances.  However, many of us are not informed about how to block people on social media.  Social blocking can be a form of self-care; the Symptoms of the Living website discuss why it can be needed https://symptomsofliving.com/blog/blocking-people-is-a-form-of-self-care/(17). Social blocking can be a bit technical. RAINN's website helps break it down for most major social media companies. https://www.rainn.org/articles/how-filter-block-and-report-harmful-content-social-media (18).

Let me share with you a quick story (Jimmy).  One day while I was visiting my friend, his child was attacked by someone on a social media platform.  The child was visibly upset, so I shared some advice. My dad always taught me that fighting was the last result, but there are times you have to put up your "dukes" and defend yourself.  I asked my friend's child what was being said, and it was nasty.  Next, I asked this child do your family and good friends say weird things like this to you on social media? The answer was no.  We spoke a little longer about the intent of the other child's comments. I then said you know what I would do? DELETE. "What do you mean, DELETE?"  Delete them from your contacts and social sites, and block their phone number.  Why keep interacting with someone disrespectful?  Seriously, one of the best things you can do is delete someone who is harmful.   My friend's child took my advice and blocked them. Later my friend got a call from the other kid's parent and wanted to know why their kid deleted her kid.

You can also use social blocking to proactively remove your data from the many internet databases or data brokers. In today's world, our information and data are sold.  Many times we freely give away to social applications or other businesses. Companies like Optery or Deleteme can scour the internet and remove your personal information from data brokers. You want to remove this information from the internet so hackers or criminals cannot use that data against you. While writing this book, we signed up for Optery and ran an initial report to find our data on the internet. You can also remove yourself from accounts you may not use anymore by using https://justdeleteme.xyz/(19) and https://justgetmydata.com/(20).

## Not All Fights are Fair

By now, you are getting a sense of how you can fight back using your weapons or tools for digital defense.  We want to alert you that fighting can be tough. Hackers are real and should not be taken lightly.  We talked earlier in the book about the white hat, the black hat, and the grey hat hackers. Remember, if you get in a tough jam, there are countless resources to help you out. Just go back and read the recent version of the Internet Crime Report by the FBI.

## The Final Social Martial Arts Move

You have done a great job and are on your way to becoming a digital defense master, but there is one last lesson, perhaps the most important lesson.  It can be more powerful than kicks, blocks, and punches.

One of the most powerful tools you have is your mind.  Yes, you!  You have the ability to think, question, and really examine the digital interaction you are having with someone.

The Federal Trade Commission has a detailed website that will help strengthen your mind.  It includes valuable information that can help you tell if someone has stolen your information.  You may visit the site at https://www.identitytheft.gov/Warning-Signs-of-Identity-Theft (21) . Here are some examples from the FTC that should be considered warning signs:

- You don't get your bills or other mail.

- You see withdrawals from your bank account that you can't explain.

- Merchants refuse your checks.

- Debt collectors call you about debts that aren't yours.

- You find unfamiliar accounts or charges on your credit report.

- Medical providers bill you for services you didn't use.

- Your health plan rejects your legitimate medical claim because the records show you've reached your benefits limit.

- A health plan won't cover you because your medical records show a condition you don't have.

- The IRS notifies you that more than one tax return was filed in your name or that you have income from an employer you don't work for.

- You get a notice that your information was compromised by a data breach at a company where you do business or have an account."

Remember, one of the best weapons you have is your mind. If you see any of the warning signs listed above. Don't engage.  You can contact the FTC directly at 877-438-4338 or online at www.usa.gov/identity-theft (22).

## Website References

We realize there are many ways and styles to cite web references. We think the easiest way is to just copy and select the URL into your browser. This book was written over two years.  Please note that we don't have control if content and links change over time.

(1) https://payback-ltd.com/blogs/12-easy-ways-to-check-if-a-website-is-legit-or-a-scam/

(2) https://www.virustotal.com/gui/home/upload

(3) https://www.urlvoid.com/

(4) https://www.lastpass.com/features/password-generator

(5) https://securitysnobs.com/Abloy/

(6) https://www.youtube.com/watch?v=vz9IPVhBUpc

(7) https://www.wired.com/story/phone-scam-phishing-finance-apps/

(8) https://www.itpro.com/security/social-engineering/361911/month-in-the-life-of-social-engineer-week-one

(9) https://www.comptia.org/content/articles/anatomy-of-a-social-engineering-attack     198

(10) https://comptiacdn.azureedge.net/webcontent/docs/default-source/research-reports/avoid-social-engineering-attacks.pdf?sfvrsn=28ea7377_2

(11) https://cybernews.com/security/rockyou2021-alltime-largest-password-compilation-leaked/

(12) https://www.informationisbeautiful.net/visualizations/worlds-biggest-data-breaches-hacks/

(13) https://www.informationisbeautiful.net/visualizations/top-500-passwords-visualized/

(14) https://haveibeenpwned.com/

(15) https://www.sysprobs.com/best-chrome-security-extensions

(16) https://www.sfweekly.com/sponsored/completely-free-reverse-phone-lookup-with-name/

(17) https://symptomsofliving.com/blog/blocking-people-is-a-form-of-self-care/

(18) https://www.rainn.org/articles/how-filter-block-and-report-harmful-content-social-media

(19) https://justdeleteme.xyz/

(20) https://justgetmydata.com/

(21) https://www.identitytheft.gov/#/Warning-Signs-of-Identity-Theft

(22) https://www.usa.gov/identity-theft

# NOTES

# Chapter 7

# A WORD TO PARENTS - PROTECTING KIDS FROM PREDATORS, TRAFFICKERS, AND BAD PEOPLE.

Why are we writing this chapter? There are really bad things that happen to kids on the Internet, and you need to be aware as a grandparent, parent, teacher, or community volunteer. There are monsters and predators lurking, waiting for the opportunity to pounce on a child through an app or gaming platform.  We will talk more about this later, as well as how human traffickers looking for young children online. Over the years, we have attended many community and law enforcement events that drill down to how people learn, watch, and connect with children.  This is by far the toughest chapter of the book.  We are going to share some things that are disturbing; however, they are very important.

**The Dark Overlord and School Kids**

We first heard about this story a few years ago. A hacker group called the Dark Overlord hacked into the Johnston Community School District in Iowa on October 2, 2017. The Des Moines Register reported that students' names, addresses, and telephone numbers were posted publicly. https://www.desmoinesregister.com/story/news/crime-and-courts/2017/10/05/dark-overlord-hacker-johnston-schools-threats/735950001/ (9)

Now I don't know about you, but if I received a text like this about my kid, I would be freaking out. In response, the school district released the following statement:

"ALERT: All Johnston Schools Cancelled October 3 Around 8 p.m. on the evening of October 2, individual students and parents within our school district received anonymous messages threatening the safety and security of our students. In an effort of caution, we will be canceling school for all students and district staff on Tuesday, October 3. All district buildings will be closed, and there is no KTC program. School district officials are working closely with the Johnston Police Department to track down the validity of the message and its source. We understand this may inconvenience parents and caretakers. However, the safety of our students – your children – is the foremost reason behind this action."

The image on this page shows the text a mom received about her child.

A Johnston mother received these text messages the night of Oct. 2, 2017. The Johnston school district closed all schools Oct. 3, as multiple parents reported receiving threatening messages and police were investigating. Explicit language has been edited out of this image. *Breana Schwitters / Special To The Register*

An article in the "Daily Republic" stated that the "Dark Overlord said on Twitter it hacked the Johnston Community School District in Iowa" and "released personal information on students, making it easy for "any child predator" to "easily acquire new targets."

**Take Away from the Dark Overlord**

Hackers are real. Now obviously, the school district and parents were upset. What was done was very disturbing. However, there are some takeaways that are very important for parents to think about:

- Does your K-12 organization have privacy protocols in place?
- How is your child's information protected?
- What kind of training do teachers receive?
- What is the protocol if a cyber attack happens?

Johnston Community is not the only school that has been hacked or ransomed. Imagine how many other hackers have accessed information and choose not to reveal their name and announce it on Twitter. This was a wake-up call to parents and schools. In a recent article in AXIOS Jason Clayworth interviewed Laura Sprague from the Johnston Community School District. The article states that the attack cost "taxpayers thousands of dollars" and that the school district's cybersecurity has doubled since the attack. Sprague also stated in this article that other hacker attacks have happened where "hackers have imitated emails of multiple school executives, including herself, in attempts to con people out of money. Some even include school logos and headers, making them harder to distinguish as fake."

- https://www.axios.com/local/des-moines/2021/09/14/johnston-public-schools-hackers-the-dark-overlord (1).

- https://www.desmoinesregister.com/story/news/crime-and-courts/2017/10/13/dark-overlord-hack-school-computers-student-information-outside-vendor-johnston-school/750730001/ (2).

- https://www.kcci.com/article/threats-force-johnston-schools-to-cancel-classes/12769814 (3).

**What Motivates Hackers to go After School Kids**

Many years ago, we interviewed a chief information officer from a K-12 school system. He shared with us that students are fair game for hackers. How could a young kid in elementary school be of interest to a hacker?

The person we interviewed explained that most kids get a social security card when they are very young. As parents, you provide this information to schools and maybe a few other organizations when needed.  Outside of that, the social security card does not get a lot of attention until the kid hits about 16 and starts thinking about college.  A hacker could easily access a young student's social security card at age 5 and go undetected for a decade.

**_Last point on why hackers get names,_ numbers, and addresses;** they are valuable to the criminal world.  Several years ago, we were attending a law enforcement conference. At the time, the organization we worked for had created a training exercise on cyber strategies to combat human trafficking. During this conference, we have a large floor space where an illicit message business was recreated to show how people can find digital and cyber clues of people getting trafficked.

A law enforcement person approached us, and we talked for a while about our training exercise at this conference.  After experiencing my company's immersive training environment, he asked why we did not have a document mill.

"A what," we said.  What is a document mill, and what does that have to do with human trafficking?  He went on to say that when law enforcement raids a human trafficking organization, they normally will find in close proximity a house (that is typically run down) with a whole bunch of technology in it and printers. He went on to point out that many of the people that are trafficked or are indendured servants will be given false driver's licenses, social security numbers, and papers.  The bottom line is that people pay for information about names, records, and addresses because they can use them to traffic people and for scams.

Library Scams are on the rise as well. We all must be aware of these tricky scams. Students and staff are targeted because every fall, students and staff return to school and need library support. The hackers prey on this timely event and use it against us. Here are two stories that investigate and describe library scams.

* https://www.proofpoint.com/us/threat-insight/post/seems-phishy-back-school-lures-target-university-students-and-staff (4)
* https://blogs.deakin.edu.au/article/dont-be-fooled-by-the-silent-librarian-scam/ (5)

If your school system does not have a disinformation incident response plan, now is the time for you to help! Ransomware as a service is available on the dark web. There are many school systems that get held for ransom after their data is stolen.

We grew up in a time when the technologies kids have access to today, simply did not exist.  Like many Gen Xers, we learned to adapt to all the new tech.  Our generation has gone from 8-track and vinyl to tape cassettes to CDs to Spotify.  Many of us remember our first computer.  We had TRS 80s and Commodore 64s. We stayed up all night playing Frogger and Space Invaders on the Atari.  Never did we dream that when we were interacting with all this technology that someone wished us harmed or could access us somehow.

Today we live in a world where kids are very connected through their smartphones and gaming platforms. There are multiple studies and surveys that have looked into how much teens are using their phones. Depending on which report you read, teens and tweens spend anywhere from 5-8 hours a day connected to the Internet of Things.  For any of you with millennials or generation Z kids, you know that texting is the preferred way to communicate.  So think about this, the proverbial "bad guys" know that kids like to use texting and messaging apps to communicate.  They understand that they spend a large amount of time connected to their devices without any kind of oversight from their parents.

Please forgive us, if it feels like we are taking a shot at parents.  We are not.  We just want you all to be aware that dangers are lurking online, and there are people who will manipulate your kid if given the chance. Let us just take a quick pause to further make this point about how much the world has changed. For any of us that grew up in the 70s, 80s, and 90s, the culture of communication has dramatically shifted from what we knew as the norm.  For example, when we were in high school, our schedule was pretty much the same every day.  After school, we would head to the practice of whatever sport we were playing.  Early on in high school, our parents would pick us up from practice at 5:30 pm. When older, we drove home from high school.  Parents expected us to be home no later than 7 pm.  If for any reason, we were going to be late, we would stop at a pay phone and call.  Once we got home, it was a quick shower, dinner, and off to study. Once all of that was done, we may get an hour or so of TV or gaming in.  If someone called the house for us, it went through the main line of our home. Typically, a family member would knock on our door and tell us who was on the phone.  This is just how things worked back then.

When my oldest son started high school, he really wanted a phone, so we said he had to get a job and pay for it, which he did.  We talk with many parents around the country who feel it is social suicide and even dangerous if their child does not have a phone.  Because of this, more and more kids have access to a device that can potentially be harmful. Check for yourself on the studies out there on how many preteens have a phone. The point is that their culture demands having a phone for access to their social communities. Parents see phones a safety device for their children. Make sure your kids know how to protect themselves digitally.

We had the privilege of hearing Opal Singleton from Millions of Kids speak. We were floored by the stats she shared.  Her website at https://millionkids.org (6) states that three thousand kids are trafficked each day.  Think about that for a minute.  THREE THOUSAND!  That stat is mind blowing.

During Opal's presentation to the law enforcement community she was addressing, she shared the following stats:

✓ 18,000 kids per day send a naked photo

✓ 9,000 kids per day are sextored

✓ 58% meet up with their predator

When we saw these stats, we immediately sent them to our family members that have younger kids.  Any app that has communication or messaging to it can expose your kid to a harmful person.

She gave example after example of how predators access kids through gaming platforms and different social sites. Opal reminded the audience that when kids share a photo online, it shares their location.  Here is how it works.  Right-click on the image of a photo. When I click on a photo, I get an option to copy the image's address.  Take the coordinates and plug them into a map.

Two items are worth reading about. I know where your cat lives is a site that shows how easy it is to use photos and metadata to gain access to people's homes and cats. https:// iknowwhereyourcatlives.com/about/ (7).  Don't F**k with

Cats: Hunting an Internet Killer https://www.netflix.com/title/81031373 (8).

We are always shocked by people who we don't really know that well but are connected to on social media and how much they share about their private lives and kids.  Many people show where they play with their kids, vacation, and eat dinner.  When a bad person gets access to information about your son or daughter, it allows them to profile them as well as make plans for how they abduct or traffic your kid.

Another example Opal gave in her discussion was targeting boys' online gaming.  A person will develop a connection with a kid online while playing a game.  After a bit of time, that person will send a nude photo of a young girl to a boy and ask for that boy to send a nude picture of himself back to "her".  This nude photo of the boy then gets distributed to a network of pedophiles on the dark web who pay to look at naked pictures of young boys.

Please take a look at the top apps that are being downloaded and ask yourself these questions:

1. Does my kid have this on their phone?  How many subscribers does this app have?

2. Who is the main audience for this app?

3. Think in terms of young girls.

4. What do they do on this site?

5. Do they post videos of themselves dancing or complain about their problems?

We cannot press upon you enough the need to beware of who and what your kids are connected to. We are not at all saying that apps and online games are bad.  If we had younger children, we would personally not allow them to connect to any game unless we reviewed it.  We would not allow games that had a messaging component to them.  We know this may make you unpopular, but please go out and read all the accounts of how some bad person when through a social app, developed a relationship, fed them a fantasy, and then trafficked them to others for sex.

Having raised and still raising a teenager, we know this can be tough.  These predators will use social engineering to shame or scare your kids.  We were recently attending a human trafficking summit and heard a trafficking survivor speak.  This person talked about how her pimp knew where her parents lived and threatened to kill them if she did not do what he said.  Many of these predators use shaming and manipulation.  Please let your son or daughter know that if they have done this, your arms are opened wide to help restore them and love them.  Don't make them feel any more ashamed than they already are.  Make sure they know they can come to you with anything.  As a family, explain to them how trafficking works and what people will do to gain access to their personal lives.

Please remember there are wolves in sheep's clothing out there looking to pounce and socially engineer your kid.  Give them the tools to fight back. We want to emphasize and make the point that you may not have a choice but to share your data to get access to schools, shopping, job onboarding, insurance, etc. Everything is online. Knowing how to protect yourself helps.

## Website References

We realize there are many ways and styles to cite web references. We think the easiest way is to just copy and select the URL into your browser. This book was written over two years.  Please note that we don't have control if content and links change over time.

(1) https://www.axios.com/local/des-moines/2021/09/14/johnston-public-schools-hackers-the-dark-overlord

(2) https://www.desmoinesregister.com/story/news/crime-and-courts/2017/10/13/dark-overlord-hack-school-computers-student-information-outside-vendor-johnston-school/750730001/

(3) https://www.kcci.com/article/threats-force-johnston-schools-to-cancel-classes/12769814

(4) https://www.proofpoint.com/us/threat-insight/post/seems-phishy-back-school-lures-target-university-students-and-staff

(5) https://blogs.deakin.edu.au/article/dont-be-fooled-by-the-silent-librarian-scam/

(6) https://millionkids.org

(7) https://iknowwhereyourcatlives.com/about/

(8) https://www.netflix.com/title/81031373

(9) https://www.desmoinesregister.com/story/news/crime-and-courts/2017/10/05/dark-overlord-hacker-johnston-schools-threats/735950001/

# Chapter 8
# SO NOW WHAT?

Before we answer this question, we want to take a quick pause and say thanks. It takes some time to read or listen to a 200-page-plus book in today's busy world. We appreciate you and hope this gave you some insights on what to avoid and how to lock down your tech and data.

There are many takeaways from this book. But the most important thing for you to remember is:

## "Cybercrime does not discriminate, be warned that anyone, anytime, and anywhere is fair game."

Right now, in America, there are 769,736 unfilled cyber jobs, according to cyber seek.org (1). This is a big increase from last year. The FBI's IC3 report recorded 847,376 complaints received by the FBI in 2021 regarding cybercrimes, with estimated costs totaling $6.9B. https://www.ic3.gov/Media/PDF/AnnualReport/2021_IC3Report.pdf?_sp=0a7b7784-1d4b-4e1a-860e-e727dc69b8bd (2). Think about this, we have a rise in the need for jobs of cyber professionals as well as cyber crimes.

The ic3.gov report shares a list of the top crimes in 2021 ranked by victims. Let's take a quick look at the top five crimes that got the most victims in 2021:

(1) **323,972** Phishing, vishing, smashing, and pharming

(2) **82,478** Non-payment, non-delivery

(3) **51,829** Personal data breach

(4) **51,629** Identity Theft

(5) **39,360** Extortion

The question was posed at the beginning of this chapter, **"So now what?"**

The answer is to take action. You don't have to implement
everything in the book all at once but start somewhere.  The
key to any journey is simply taking the first step.  Here are
some first steps you can take:

- ☑ **Phone-**Your mobile phone probably goes everywhere
  with you. It comes on workouts, family gatherings, car
  drives, trips, and pretty much all of your social
  engagements. We provided you with some tactics in the
  Digital Defense and Social Martial Arts chapter on how to
  digitally block, punch and kick. Take time each day and
  make sure your phone is secure. You may be surprised
  that you have been allowing access to your data,
  camera, and mic. We also shared with you some apps
  you can use to protect your phone.

- ☑ **Predators** - They are a real threat. Educate your kids,
  nieces, nephews, and students on how to deal with
  digital predators, and about their privacy when
  communicating with strangers online. The FBI has a site
  that delves into this at https://www.fbi.gov/how-we-can-
  help-you/safety-resources/scams-and-safety/common-
  scams-and-crimes/sextortion. Please visit this site and
  take time to understand how these predator work.
  Remember, it is important to know who is influencing
  your kids. President Biden said in a tweet from March 1,

2022, "We must hold social media platforms accountable for the national experiment they're conducting on our children. It is time to strengthen privacy protections, ban targeted advertising to your children, and demand tech companies stop collecting personal data on our children."

- ☑ **Your House -** With many of us working remotely and spending a large part of our day in browsers accessing information for our work, it is really important to ensure your home and the points of connectivity are secured. For many of us, we make sure to lock our cars and the doors to our homes every night, but we do not take the same advice for our devices. We list out several things you should do to lock your tech down back in the chapter on your digital dust.

- ☑ **Social Engineering-** Your call to action is to be aware of other people and your surroundings at all times. Whether you are in person, online, or on a mobile call out in public, there is a possibility of you being manipulated. Just this week, an article was published on how social engineers target people who post a new job and pretend to be representatives from the new company to gain access and scam folks starting a new job.

- ☑ **Chat GPT-** In December 2022, a new AI tool called ChatGPT went viral  https://chat.openai.com/chat  (4). People need to be aware that cyber security and

ChatGPT AI has the potential to help professionals and others defend against future cybercrimes. This tool has the potential to answer complex questions as if it was human. According to the website Chat.openai, "We've trained a model called ChatGPT which interacts in a conversational way. The dialogue format makes it possible for ChatGPT to answer follow-up questions, admit its mistakes, challenge incorrect premises, and reject inappropriate requests. ChatGPT is a sibling model to InstructGPT, which is trained to follow an instruction in a prompt and provide a detailed response." The world now has a tool that could help anyone write code, write papers, and learn about anything in detail from the comfort of their own device! There will be many challenges and considerations regarding this tool. For example, it has the potential to plagiarize or be used inappropriately in other ways. We think of it as an idea thesaurus and can be a great tool if we teach people to use it for learning not cheating. According to searchenginejournal.com (5), " It's a revolutionary technology because it's trained to learn what humans mean when they ask a question. Many users are awed at its ability to provide human-quality responses, inspiring the feeling that it may eventually have the power to disrupt how humans interact with computers and change how information is retrieved."

Our journey and time together are coming to a close. We have included a glossary of terms in the back of this book . We also interviewed each other so you can learn more about why we wrote this book and what our favorite chapters are.

Our friends at Temple University have some outstanding resources for anyone to use.  Please visit https:// sites.temple.edu/care/resources/ (3). Additionally, below are links to two academic papers written in 2022 regarding social engineering and psychology!

- https://www.mdpi.com/2076-3417/12/12/6042/pdf?version=1655208887  (6)

- https://www.frontiersin.org/articles/10.3389/fpsyg.2020.01755/full (7)

Wishing you cyber peace, health, and happiness!

Henry and Jimmy

## Website References

We realize there are many ways and styles to cite web references. We think the easiest way is to just copy and select the URL into your browser. This book was written over two years.  Please note that we don't have control if content and links change over time.

(1)https://www.cyberseek.org/heatmap.html

(2) https://www.ic3.gov/Media/PDF/AnnualReport/ 2021_IC3Report.pdf?_sp=0a7b7784-1d4b-4e1a-860e-e727dc69b8bd

(3) https://sites.temple.edu/care/resources/

(4) https://chat.openai.com/chat

(5)  searchenginejournal.com

(6) https://www.mdpi.com/2076-3417/12/12/6042/pdf? version=1655208887

(7) https://www.frontiersin.org/articles/10.3389/ fpsyg.2020.01755/full

# NOTES

# GLOSSARY

J ust a quick note on the glossary. You will notice that the glossary is not alphabetized. We listed definitions as they are presented in each chapter.

**Phishing** is an email that comes to your inbox that is designed to trick you into opening a link or to get you to perform an action.

**Smishing** is when someone is getting socially engineered through text messaging.

**Tailgate** (walk in the building as someone else walks out, not needing a security badge to swipe to gain access

**Cyber Attack** An unwanted person(s) accesses information from a person, business, school, or government organization digitally. Think of this as someone breaking into a computer.

**Spear Phishing** targets a specific group or type of user, such as a system administrator.

Whaling are attacks that target a CEO, CFO, CISO, and CTO.

**Vishing** has the same intention but uses a voice call for the attack.

 **Pharming** a portmanteau of the words "phishing" and "farming", is an online scam similar to phishing, where a website's traffic is manipulated, and confidential information is stolen. Please revisit these websites at: https://www.trendmicro.com/en_us/what-is/phishing/types-of-phishing.html#vishing-tm-anchor  and https://usa.kaspersky.com/resource-center/definitions/pharming.

**White Hat Hackers** White Hat hacker is a good guy who uses his (or her) capabilities to damage your organization - but only hypothetically. Instead, the real purpose is to uncover security failings in your system in order to help you safeguard your business from dangerous hackers.

**IC3** The United States Federal Bureau of Investigation (FBI) Internet Crime Complaint Center (IC3) issues an annual report on cyber breaches.  Please read this to keep up on what is happening around the USA at www.ic3.gov.

**Insider Threat** There are two kinds of insider threats: employees and subcontractors. These are people that have access to technology or your organization's building.

**Ransomware** is software that will prevent your computer systems from working. Once on your system, you will get a message from someone that you have to pay money to get control back of your computer.

**<u>Social Engineering</u>** Think of social engineering as the ability to hack or manipulate a person using things in their environment.


**<u>Zoom Bombing</u>** When everyone went home to work and do school remotely in March of 2020, zoom became a platform that everyone used to communicate.  Sometimes, intruders would break into a meeting.  Thus the term zoom bombing was created.

**<u>Open Source Intelligence (OSINT)</u>** is gathering information and data that is publicly available. There are sources and techniques people can utilize to gain information on a target or mark.


**<u>Sock Puppet</u>** is when social engineers use fictional accounts and fake personas. Many social engineers use fictional accounts and fake personas.   - When social engineers use fictional accounts and fake personas to trick someone.

**<u>Generative Adversarial Networks (GAN),</u>** we can learn how to create realistic-looking fake versions of almost anything we need.

**Albert Mehrabian 7-35-55 communications rules.** The 7-38-55 rule is a concept concerning the communication of emotions. The rule states that 7 percent of meaning is communicated through spoken word, 38 percent through tone of voice, and 55 percent through body language.

**Deepfakes** The 21st century's answer to Photoshopping, deepfakes use a form of artificial intelligence called deep learning to make images of fake events, hence the name deepfake.

**Virtual Private Network (VPN)** VPN stands for "Virtual Private Network" and describes the opportunity to establish a protected network connection when using public networks. VPNs encrypt your internet traffic and disguise your online identity. This makes it more difficult for third parties to track your activities online and steal data. The encryption takes place in real time.

**Bluebugging** is where a hacker will access your phone's information via the process when two devices connect together.

**Bluejacking** is when you get messages from a source you do not know. The key here is they are just sending messages.

**Bluesnarfing** is when someone gets on your phone and takes information.

**Cookie:** In the tech world, a cookie is basically a file that stores information about you, such as a password.

**MFA FATIGUE** MFA Fatigue attack is when a threat actor runs a script that attempts to log in with stolen credentials over and over, causing what feels like an endless stream of MFA push requests to be sent to the account's owner's mobile device.

**Secure Texting** is using text apps that use encryption for messaging.

**USB blocker** USB blocker will stop unwanted data access of your information from a public port.

**SSIDs** or (Service Set Identifier) is the name of the Wi-Fi network.

**2FA** Two Factor Authentication is a technology where you get a message on your personal device to ensure it is you accessing certain data.

**OTP** one-time password OTP systems provide a mechanism for entering a network or service using a unique password that can only be used once

**Jailbreaking** is exploiting the defect of a locked-down electronic device to install software other than what the manufacturer has made available for that device.

**Robocall** A robocall is a phone call that uses a computerized autodialer to deliver a pre-recorded message as if from a robot. The service is also associated to be prone to scams.

**<u>Password Manager</u>** software to manage all of your passwords.

# Henry

# INTERVIEW

We have both dedicated three years of our lives to writing this book. We thought it would be a good idea to interview each other on our takeaways from the book. Jimmy (JB) will now interview Henry (HD) on the book.

1. JB: Henry, why did you decide to write the book?
   HD "My passion is sharing knowledge to help others protect themselves from social engineering and basic digital literacy!"

2. JB: Why is this book different than other social engineering books in the marketplace?
   HD "We provide interesting stories that resonate with everyday humans. We will show you how to apply these tactics to your personal life. Protecting yourself from digital harm is a must in this day and age, and we supply great insight in this book on how social engineering affects us all in the modern world."

3.  JB: What would you say if you had a minute or less to explain this book to someone?

HD: "Open to any part of the book, I guarantee you will find something that sparks your interest, and you will want to read more about the topic."

4.  JB: Give us your top takeaways from the book.

HD "My top takeaways are that people naturally trust others. This can be a huge problem. Protecting yourself from social engineering needs to be discussed at the dinner table. Be suspicious, think before you click, and never rush into an email or phone call until you trust and verify the source! Digital defense is an art, and you must practice becoming proficient!"

5.  JB: What is your favorite chapter in the book?

HD "Chapter 5 Click and the Digital dust describes some useful points and engaging stories!

6.  JB: How can people continue the discussion with you and learn "social-martial arts" from us?

HD "Follow us on Twitter, go online reach out to us with your stories on LinkedIn or Twitter!" Be mindful of others around you.

Jimmy

# INTERVIEW

A s we conclude this book. Henry has a few questions for Jimmy:

## 1. Jimmy, share with the reader why you decided to write this book.

Several years ago, Henry and I were in Vegas for a hacking conference. This conference has a reputation that if you don't have your stuff locked down, it may get hacked. Many people advised me not to bring credit cards or my phone as it was fair game for the hacking community. Henry told me before the conference that you are a marketing person and you really need your phone to do all the stuff for your job. I will make sure you and your phone are safe.  I remember HD taking me to the wall of sheep to show me that my phone was safe.  Henry taught me how to lock down and protect my tech.  I remember asking why doesn't everyone know how to do this stuff.

As COVID-19 started, we saw social engineering scams galore everywhere and realized that we needed to create a guide that anyone could understand and give them tactics to protect themselves.  Just the other day, President Biden got federal leaders and industry together to discuss the increased threats facing America and our citizens.  Threats are real. You are now informed. Go forth and lock down your tech.

## 2.  What is your hope for the everyday person reading this book?

In short, they can learn to stop a social engineering attack and lock down their tech.  Especially, kids, there are all kinds of creepers out there that prey on young girls and boys.  I hope parents and teachers take chapter seven to heart. Please make sure your kids are safe. There are some really dangerous and gnarly things that happen to kids online. Learn to thwart the attacks of the wolf in sheep's clothes.

3.  **You really wanted to make a book for all ages.  From senior citizens to kids, what are some of the important takeaways?**

We have several sections of the book for kids and seniors. For seniors, don't think you are not technical. Take time to learn. Your generation was blessed with great common sense. Use that to make good decisions when you interact online.  Remember, people will use what you are scared about to manipulate.  Also, if you get an email that you think is real, take time to validate the legitimacy of the request and attack.

For all students in school that have grown up digitally, listen to me on this. You don't know everything, and neither do I. However, I know for a fact that people will prey on you in messaging apps and gaming platforms.  Why? Because they can make money trafficking you?  Please take my comments here seriously.  I have listened to many trafficking victims that tell the story of how they met someone online. That person gave them hope or offered them something they wanted (like a modeling career), and then one day, everything changed, and they were in a very dangerous and scary place.  As a dad, let me tell you that there is nothing I would not do for kids, no matter what they did. Most parents' love is unconditional.  If you did something stupid and someone is trying to blackmail you, get help.  Don't be ashamed.

**4. Do you have a favorite chapter or section of the book?** I put my heart and soul into this book. This is a hard question for me to answer, but I am going with the chapter on Digital Defense and Social Martial Arts.

**5. What's next for you and Henry?**
We are gonna rest.  We both have day jobs, so this book was done over late nights and weekends. For the book specifically, we are open to helping and training folks about all the stuff in the book. Just connect with us after you have read the book.

Personally, after I rest, I am going to start on another writing project. This is my fourth book, and I am looking to try my hand at a different writing medium.  I am also working on a side project with my restorative justice project, "Freedom Shift," to help inspire kids who are in really tough life circumstances on how to transition into a career being a white hat hacker.  We are helping kids that don't have a ton of money and have been dealt some bad cards to learn some basic cyber skills and transition to getting an associate's degree in cybersecurity from a community college.  For real, if you have an AA and cybersecurity certification, you are employable.  A career in tech can change any socioeconomic position for the better.

Outside of the book, we are friends. Henry is a super-funny, kind person, and I consider myself blessed to have him as a friend. So we are gonna keep getting together and hanging out.

**Endorsements:**

"This book 'Social Engineering and Digital Defense Survival Guide for the Everyday Person' is an excellent resource for anyone looking to improve their online safety and security. The authors Henry and Jimmy, do a great job of explaining complex concepts in an easy-to-understand way. The book is full of practical tips and strategies for protecting yourself from social engineering and other online threats. Whether you are a beginner or have some experience with online security, this book is a must-read for anyone who wants to stay safe in today's digital world."
**Jorge Avila, Security Specialist, NorCal President of Tech-Latino**

"Jimmy and Henry's book is a must-read for anyone that engages with the internet or has a mobile phone, from senior citizens to students. This book will teach you about the threats and ways to protect you, your family, and your community."
**Mark Moreno, Director of Enterprise Architecture, CCISP, CCSP**

"I've known Jimmy Baker for about 20 years, and there are a few things I can say for certain about him: he is a voracious student of many things, especially things involving technology. The other thing that has been apparent to me since we met is his intense concern for people and their well-being. This book brings to the fore both of these aspects of Jimmy Baker. Given the times we live in, the timing for a comprehensive book like this could not be better."

**Mark Amtower, Preeminent Marketing and LinkedIn Advisor to the Most Successful Small, Mid-tier and Large Government Contractors, Radio Host, and Author**

"The Social Engineer and Digital Defense is a must-read! For everyday people who aren't in the cyber security field, understanding all of the different threats and scams that can affect our personal lives may seem overwhelming. As technology becomes increasingly intertwined with our day-to-day lives, we need all the help we can get to stay safe from cyber attacks and social engineering.

Henry and Jimmy have done a fantastic job crafting a book that is engaging and understandable for everyone, from students to senior citizens. Their conversational tone and straightforward explanations make what have traditionally been confusing and scary topics feel so much easier to grasp. Full of practical advice and valuable information."
**Christopher Patrick, Author of *Leading to Change***

"As our lives become further immersed in the digital realm, a breach of your data could have lifelong consequences. This book contains the blueprint for defending yourself against the multitude of hackers, con-artists, and scammers that roam the Internet."
**Eric Escobar, Hacker**